American Government

not for teenagers only

by

Earl H. Bourland

ISBN-0-9609350-2-9

Earl H. Bourland has also authored
How to Read A Mine Map
and
A Course In Coal Mine Ventilation
Both publications are now out of print.

Illustrated
Copyright © Earl H. Bourland 1988

ISBN-0-9609350-2-9

First Edition
Published by Management Club Consultants
P.O. Box 460028
Garland, Texas 75046

To
Aldean
Kent
Gary
Jason
Christopher

THOSE WHO HELPED

I feel indebted to:

Sherry Gritch—Dallas, Texas
   Ms. Gritch is a professional art director. She has taken my rough sketches and copy and, alone, made them into the attractive book you see. Without her expertise from rough copy through printing, this book would not exist.

Jamie Johnson—Dallas, Texas
   Jamie Johnson is a professional reporter and editor. Her guidance and editing has been invaluable in making this a quality book.

Winona M. Smith—Sandusky, Ohio
   Winona (an ex-school teacher and administrative secretary) has a professional typing and secretarial service. She has worked with me from the beginning. She knows how to do manuscripts and is an excellent typist. Most of all, I appreciated her ability to re-arrange my work so it looks good.

James A. Edwards—Sandusky, Ohio
   Mr. Edwards has taught American Government at Margaretta High School (Ohio) for fifteen years. He is a graduate of Bowling Green State University, Bowling Green, Ohio, with a master's degree in education. When the manuscript was complete, I sent it to Mr. Edwards. He reviewed the text, the sketches and sketch descriptions, marking what did not look right to him. He knows government. I'm glad I found him.

ABOUT THIS BOOK

WRITTEN BY
A fellow who has helped his kids with their homework.

WRITTEN BECAUSE
Textbooks on government sometimes are hard to understand.

WRITTEN
In the language that most of us use at the supper table every night.

YOU COULD SAY
This book is a recording of talks to a teenager on how our government works. Thumb through, read a little; you'll see the difference. The sketches, some with two colors, were necessary when explaining about Democrats and Republicans. Supper table talk enables a teenager to keep his mind on what is being said. Government is not hard to understand. The way it is presented occasionally can turn a student off. Once you lose him, it's hard to get him back on track.

TABLE OF CONTENTS

ments of the colonies, states and the United States were just about alike. In other words, each is made up of three parts, each part with a different kind of job to do. This chapter explains the three parts with sketches.

Few things in the study of our government are as confusing to the beginner as the names our two groups of lawmakers have been saddled with; i.e., upper house and lower house. The sketches should plant the proper picture in the mind of the student.

The names mentioned above are executive, legislative and judicial. The same names are used in the government of the colonies, states and United States. The words and the sketch in this chapter should provide a lasting understanding.

This chapter tells us how the colonists acquired the know-how that enabled them to write our Constitution. You could say two of the colonies were governed by the people, three were partially governed by the people, and eight were mostly governed by the king. When the representatives met in Philadelphia to write our Constitution, their varied experiences had taught them what to look out for. The three sketches should contribute to the students' understanding.

To get the most from this chapter, the student should witness a trial in session. The sketch should contribute to the understanding.

This chapter explains how the colonies begin to reach out and get acquainted with their neighbors. It is the beginning of nationalism.

England had just finished seven years of war. She needed money. The colonies were pressured and were beginning to look to each other for help. They were beginning to realize that there is strength in numbers.

The colonies needed two things:
(1) to pull away from England,
(2) to establish a national government
This chapter also tells of the events that were slowly separating them from England. All the while, they were moving toward a national government.

Since many of their leaders had gone

up our government. A sketch with this
chapter shows the parts we have studied
and what is yet to be studied. It is hoped
(as an example) that as we learn about
the Senate, we can keep in mind that it
is part of the three parts that make up
our government.

This chapter explains what the House of
Representatives is, what it is for and
what is required to be a member. A
sketch shows some of the special re-
sponsibilities of the group.

One sketch shows what takes place
when the Republicans are the majority
party. One sketch shows what takes
place when the Democrats have the
most members in the House of Representatives.

The above words have always been confusing to the beginner. To make it less
confusing, we are using a make-believe
state with only 27 residents. It is divided into three districts (apportionments)
of nine residents each. One sketch
shows what apportionment is. One
sketch shows what gerrymandering is.

CHAPTER 1

What Is Government?

If you were starting from scratch and wanted to know how to build a house, the first thing you would ask about would be the materials. Well, the same thing applies to our government. When you think about it, it's simple enough. It's people. What kind of people? It's people who believe in treating others fairly. But that's not all. It's people who demand fair treatment in return. Are Americans that way? The answer is yes. Are we born that way? For the most part we are. Just about everyone has a strong sense of fair play.

Our sense of fair play is strengthened in the home. A tiny baby soon learns that if he yells, he will be fed. Along with that, he learns something else. He learns that no matter how loud he yells he sometimes has to wait. Whether he is breast fed or bottle fed, the mother can't always get to him right away. He learns little by little that he is not always in full control.

Before long that youngster is promoted to the high chair. He sits at the table with the rest of the family. Can he throw food? Absolutely not. Dad sees to that. Dad says, "How'd you like for us to throw food at you? You can sit by yourself in the kitchen for a while."

After a while, he gets a tricycle. He soon learns what possession is. He can't take the other kid's bike without permission. On the other hand, he learns that what's his is his, and the other kid is not to touch it unless he says so.

On and on we grow into men and women. Just let us learn that

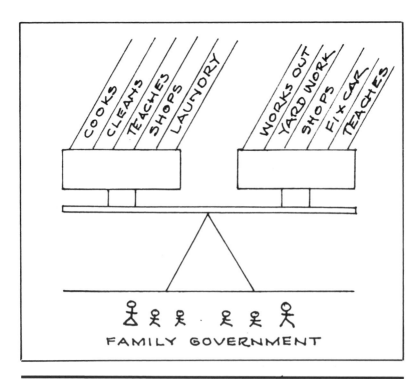

Sketch 1.   The first lesson in government starts at home. The laws that govern are there, but they are unwritten. Of course, no two families have the same rules to go by. However, all families have one thing — that's balance. Although not perfect at all times, a reasonable balance always exists. All of us can look back and remember the little unspoken rules that kept the family together.

someone on the job is making more money doing the same work. We can't take that. It has to be fair. You could say that fair play is, by nature and early training, deeply embedded in all of us. That's why a workable system of government is so difficult to put together.

One of the simple forms of government is the family — the husband, wife and the children. (See sketch 1) There are rules, unwritten rules. A sense of fairness is understood. Success depends on give and take. It has to be balanced. Not exactly at all times, but within reason.

CHAPTER 2

The Constitution

The United States Constitution is a set of rules. You could say it's a book of rules. Well, not really. A pamphlet of rules is more like it. In any case, it tells how our government should operate. We have pictured the U.S. Constitution with a baseball rule book because their uses are similar. (See sketch 2) Baseball is played every day all over the country with no thought of the rule book. However, if something comes up, it's there. It's there if you need it. The same thing applies to our government. It operates every day. No one thinks of the Constitution. It, too, is a set of rules that can be referred to if something comes up.

A baseball rule book can be changed. No doubt about that. It's not easy. There has to be a good reason. A lot of people have to agree to it. The same thing applies to the Constitution. As times and conditions change, the U.S. rule book can be changed. A lot of people have to agree to it. However, when a change is necessary, it can be made.

Since the Constitution (the little pamphlet) is the very basis for how the United States is governed, there is a tendency to exclaim what a great document it is. However, that would not do any good. It would be like telling you how good apples taste. We can say this: it's been around for over two hundred years, and it works.

Note: As mentioned above, our rule book can be changed. Those changes are called amendments. In other words, if a mother made out a list for her son to take to the grocery and it contained "soap,

Sketch 2. There is a rule book that tells how to play baseball. There is a rule book that tells how the United States is to be governed. It is called the United States Constitution.

starch and sugar," and just before he left she said, "Wait a minute, I forgot to list coffee and tea." You could speak of "coffee and tea" as amendments. Coffee would be Amendment No. 1 and Tea would be Amendment No. 2.

CHAPTER 3

The People

To the student: The purpose of this chapter is to tell a little something about the people who wrote the United States Constitution.

It wouldn't make much sense to get involved in the study of our government without a pretty good picture in our minds of the people who put it together. They are called colonists. A colonist is a person who belongs to a colony. A colony is a group of people who settle in a new country but remain somewhat loyal to the old country. They came from several countries, but most of them came from England. There were thirteen colonies. (See sketch 3) They were located in the northeastern part of what is now the United States. There were perhaps a couple of million of these people. It's been two hundred years since they put the final touches on the system of government we are now using. However, colonies were in existence perhaps one hundred fifty years before that.

It was good business for the King (and England) to have the colonies. A new country. Lots of things that England needed, the colonies could furnish, including farm products and some manufactured goods. On the other hand, England gave the colonies a feeling of security. A country with an army to protect them if need be. Then, too, there was loyalty. Many of the colonists' parents and grandparents came from England.

Another thing that everyone could wonder about was, why did the people leave the old country to join the colonies? That question can best be answered by thinking about the way we are today. Why

THE THIRTEEN COLONIES

Sketch 3.   The above sketch shows the thirteen colonies that started our country. The success of any country pretty well depends on how the people get along with each other. That's government.

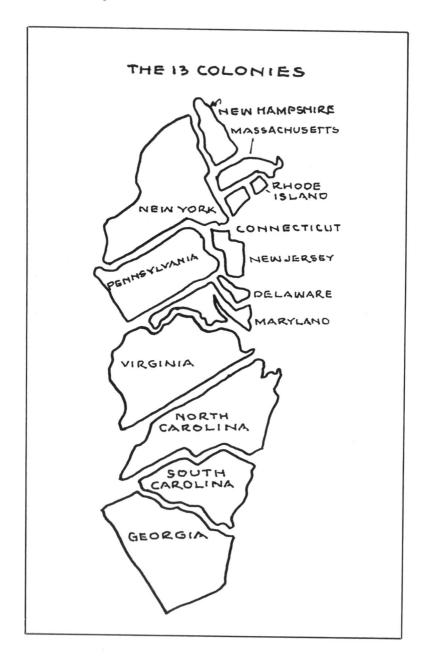

THE 13 COLONIES

Sketch 3A. This sketch shows the original 13 colonies. They were: New Hampshire, Massachusetts, Rhode Island, New York, Connecticut, New Jersey, Pennsylvania, Delaware, Maryland, Virginia, North Carolina, South Carolina and Georgia.

do people move from one place to another here in the States? Many reasons exist: job hunting, joining relatives, satisfying a roving nature and so on.

Now, the main question. What were the people like? They were very much like we are today; mostly people with children trying to make a living the best way they could.

CHAPTER 4

Things
To Understand

All of us have heard the word "lawmaker." What does it mean? Someone who makes laws? That's close, but not quite right. Here's why. Lawmaking is not a one-man job. You could say it's a process requiring several people. Before a law can be passed, it has to be presented for all the lawmakers to see. Each lawmaker has an opportunity to think it over, study it, debate, research and the like. Finally, he has a chance to vote on it. If it gets enough votes, it becomes a law.

In some colonies, one group of men made the laws. (See sketch 4) For a law to be passed, it had to be okayed by a majority of men in the group. They were spoken of as "the assembly." The dictionary definition of assembly is "called together."

In some of the colonies, two groups made the laws. (See sketch 5) For a law to be passed, it had to be okayed by a majority in each group. The groups did not meet in the same room.

Now, a question. Why two groups? Do two groups make better laws than one group? Not necessarily. Sometimes just one group is used and it seems to work just as well. When two groups are used, there is usually a difference in their background, area they represent, profession, or perhaps in the way they are selected to be lawmakers. All of which has a tendency to promote independent thinking when it becomes time to vote.

As an example, suppose, just suppose that one group of lawmakers was composed mostly of bankers and the other group was made up mostly of farmers. It is obvious that each group would look

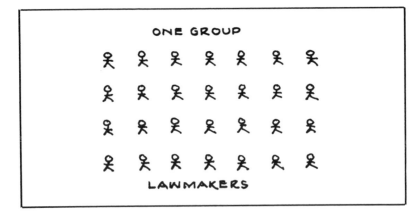

ONE GROUP

LAWMAKERS

Sketch 4.   In some states and some countries just one group of people makes the laws. It seems to work.

TWO GROUPS
LAWMAKERS

Sketch 5.   Each group pretty well keeps to itself. They are separate organizations.

at some proposed laws from a different viewpoint. When this happens, the law has to be changed so that it is acceptable to both sides. That's part of the lawmaker's job. ''Give and take'' are parts of the lawmaking process.

CHAPTER 5

How The Colonies Were Governed

Since there were thirteen colonies, it is obvious that there would be some difference in the way they were governed. However, the basic setup in all of them was pretty much the same.

They all had written rules to go by. That is to say that each colony had some form of a constitution. Some had their own ideas and wrote their own. Some took their ideas from England.

Each of the colonies was governed by:

a. **A Governor**
His job was to see that the laws were obeyed. He also tended to the colony's business. You could say he was the head man. He was the boss. He had some helpers. They were called his staff. (See sketch 6)

b. **Lawmakers**
Their job was to make laws. (See sketch 7)

c. **The Courts**
There were three levels of courts in the colonies. (See sketch 8)

1. **Justice of the Peace**. He handled minor cases. As an example:
someone kicked by another man's mule; neighbors quarreling over fence lines.

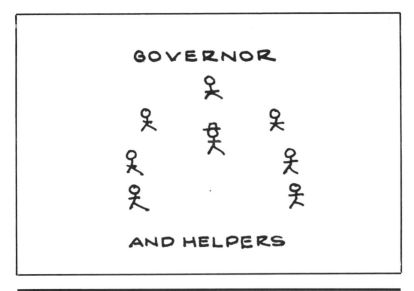

Sketch 6. In most of the colonies, the governors were appointed by the King.

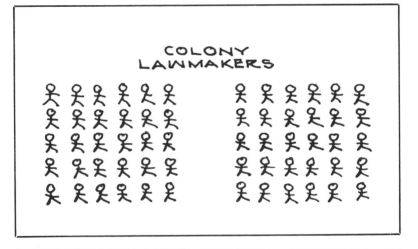

Sketch 7. They made the rules that they were to live by.

COURT STRUCTURE
(COLONIES)

FIRST LEVEL
JUSTICE OF THE PEACE

HE WAS USUALLY ELECTED IN RURAL AREAS AND SMALL TOWNS. ONLY MINOR CASES WERE HANDLED.

大 - JUSTICE

SECOND LEVEL
COUNTY COURTS

MANY CASES INVOLVED BIG FINES AND IMPRISONMENT.

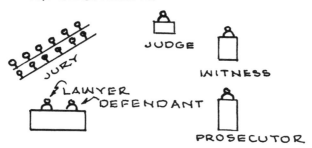

JURY

JUDGE

WITNESS

LAWYER

DEFENDANT

PROSECUTOR

THIRD LEVEL
COURTS OF APPEALS

THERE WAS USUALLY ONLY ONE COURT OF APPEALS IN EACH COLONY. IT HEARD ONLY THE MOST SERIOUS CASES.

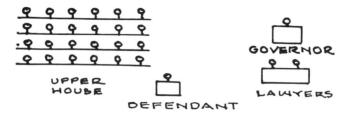

UPPER HOUSE

DEFENDANT

GOVERNOR

LAWYERS

Sketch 8. **The sketch at left represents a court scene. It shows the judge, witness, jury, defense lawyer, prosecutor, defendant (man on trial) and the spectators.**

2. **County Courts**. They handled all but the most serious cases.

3. **Court of Appeals**. This court was at the top of the system. It was at times handled by the governor and one of the groups of lawmakers. Also, some cases were handled by the King.

CHAPTER 6

Naming Lawmaking Groups

Note to the student: Sometimes simple things are confusing and hard to understand by what they are called. That's what happened to the two groups of people who make our laws. An effort is made in this chapter to make the names a little more understandable. (See sketches 10 & 11)

As previously mentioned, most of the colonies were represented by two groups. You could say each group was an organization of its own. No proposed bill could become a law until it was okayed by each group. So, in order to distinguish each of the groups from the other, they had to be named. Well, one of them could have been named "a" and the other one "b." That would have been fine. No confusion. Easy to remember. Or, to give another example, one of the groups could have been called "Group 1" and the other referred to as "Group 2." That would have been fine. No confusion. Easy to remember.

However, it wasn't done that way. Way back there a long time ago some fellow came along and decided to call one of the groups "Upper House" and the other "Lower House."

Now, let us hasten to explain that the words "upper" and "lower" have nothing to do with elevation of the two groups. Also, the word "house" does not refer to a dwelling, a home, place to live or anything of the kind.

So, let us remember that "Upper House" means "a group of lawmakers. "Lower House" means "a group of lawmakers." It's that simple.

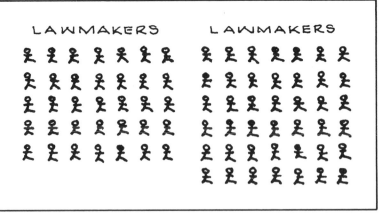

Sketch 10.   The sketch above represents two groups of lawmakers.

LAWMAKERS   LAWMAKERS

UPPER HOUSE

LOWER HOUSE

Sketch 11.   Now . . . to help us get a little more accustomed to using the names "Upper House" and "Lower House" we are (above) showing a sketch of each of the two groups. You will note we have in each sketch retained the name "lawmaker," which they still are. We have added "Upper House" and "Lower House" below. Nothing has changed. They are still two groups of lawmakers.

CHAPTER 7

Names For Governor, Lawmakers, Courts

We have previously mentioned that the colonies were governed by:
a. a governor
b. lawmakers
c. the courts.

The three words (governor, lawmaker and courts) are easy to understand. They give us a pretty good idea of what the government of the colonies was like.

However, that was not true of everyone. Way back there a long time ago some fellow came along and dressed up the above-mentioned government jobs in a little fancier language. He called the governor (and his staff): **the executive branch.**

He called the lawmakers: **the legislative branch.**

He called the courts: **the judicial branch.**

Nothing has changed. The parts of the government are the same except each part now has another name. (See sketch 12)

Some people will say "governor," some will say "executive branch."

Some people will say "lawmakers," some will say "legislative branch."

Some people will say "courts," some will say "judicial branch."

Definitions:

Executive means "capable of performing." Legislative means "having power to make laws." Judiciary means "pertinent to the courts of law."

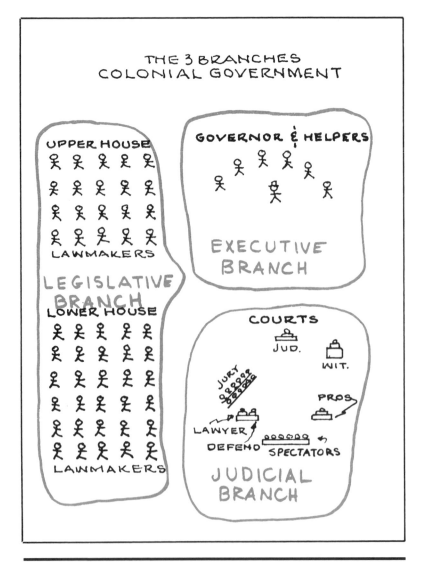

Sketch 12.   The legislative branch is sometimes confusing because it is made up of two groups of lawmakers. Since both are lawmakers, and the word "legislative" means lawmaking, the two (taken together) are termed "the legislative branch."

CHAPTER 8

How The Colonists Were Ruled

Let's start with a question. Why should we have any interest in how the colonists were ruled? Here's why. It's to get a better understanding of how they acquired the know-how to write the rules by which we live (our Constitution).

Let us get in mind the situation as it existed at the time. You could say they were like thirteen little countries living by themselves. They had little or no connection with each other. This meant that experience was available from thirteen different governments when the colonists wrote our book of rules. The Constitution was written behind closed doors and little or nothing is known as to what was said and who said it. However, it is reasonable to feel that these colonists had a lot to say about the advantages of having elected lawmakers and officials.

As mentioned before, the basic setup of each colony was pretty much the same. There were:

the governor,
the lawmakers and
the courts.

In two of the colonies, the lawmakers and governors got along well with the people. (See sketch 13)

In three of the colonies, the lawmakers and governors got along just fairly well with the people. (See sketch 14)

In eight of the colonies, it was almost a continuous quarrel. (See sketch 15)

CHARTER COLONIES

RHODE ISLAND AND CONNECTICUT

ELECTED BY PEOPLE

UPPER HOUSE

GOVERNOR
ELECTED BY
LOWER HOUSE

ELECTED BY
PEOPLE

LOWER HOUSE

Sketch 13.   Rhode Island and Connecticut were called "Charter Colonies" because an agreement between the colony and the King was stated on a piece of paper called a charter.

You will note from the sketch the following:

Upper House — elected by people

Lower House — elected by people

Governor — elected by Lower House.

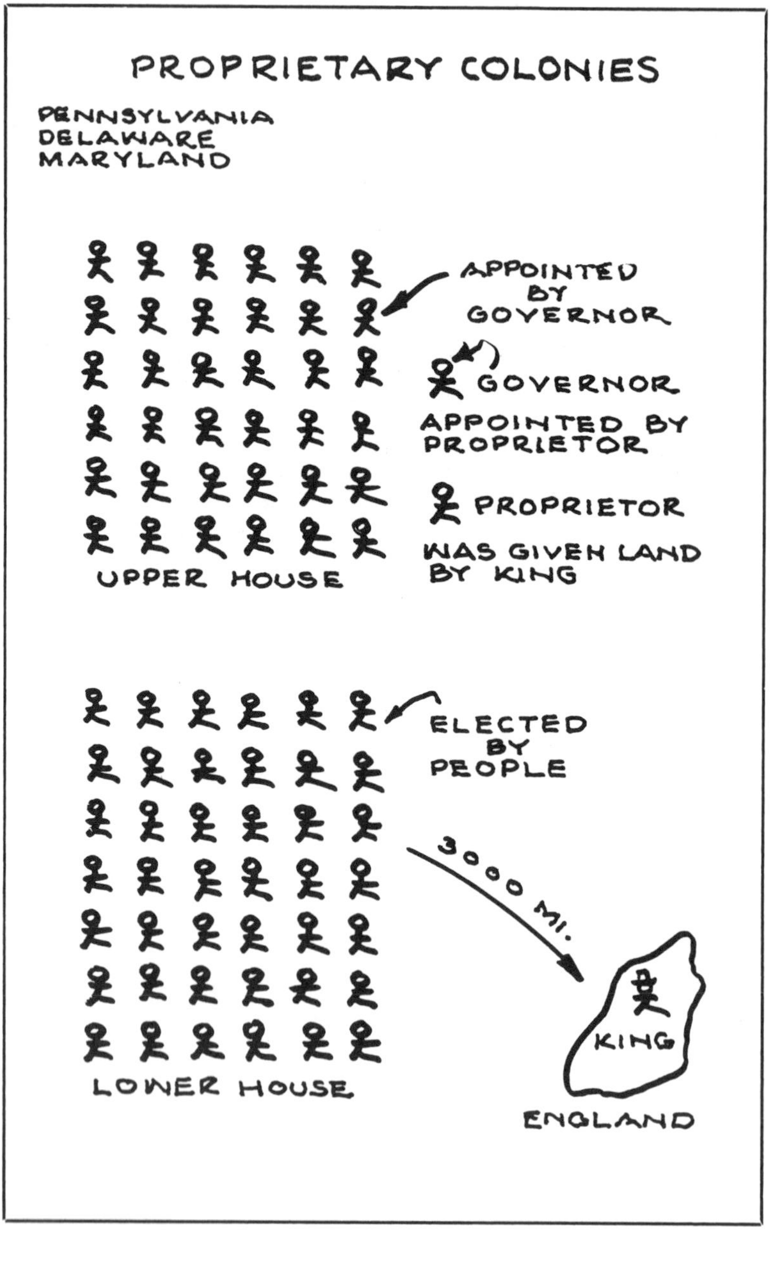

PROPRIETARY COLONIES

PENNSYLVANIA
DELAWARE
MARYLAND

APPOINTED BY GOVERNOR

GOVERNOR

APPOINTED BY PROPRIETOR

PROPRIETOR

WAS GIVEN LAND BY KING

UPPER HOUSE

ELECTED BY PEOPLE

3000 MI.

KING

LOWER HOUSE

ENGLAND

Sketch 14.   The sketch to the left is headed Proprietary Colonies. Let's be sure we understand what that means. The word "proprietor" means *owner of land*. The word "proprietary" means *pertaining to the owner of land*. Pennsylvania, Delaware and Maryland were ruled by governors who were appointed by owners of the land. So as a result, some writer referred to the three colonies as the *proprietary colonies*. The name stayed with them.

The proprietary colonies were ruled by governors who were appointed by owners of the land. The land was given to the owner by the King. Of course, this made the landowner obligated to put pressure on the governor to carry out the King's orders. Then, since the governor was given his job by the proprietor, he was obligated to pass the King's orders on to the members of the Upper House. The members of the Upper House were appointed by the governor. Consequently, what the King wanted came first when the Lower House passed on some ruling and tried to get it through the Upper House.

Note: There were periods in which some of the above colonies had only one lawmaking body.

ROYAL COLONIES

NEW HAMPSHIRE, NEW YORK, GEORGIA, NORTH CAROLINA, SOUTH CAROLINA, NEW JERSEY, VIRGINIA, MASSACHUSETTS.

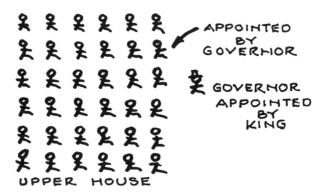

APPOINTED BY GOVERNOR

GOVERNOR APPOINTED BY KING

UPPER HOUSE

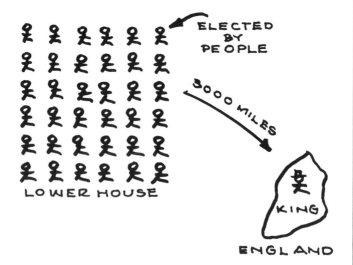

ELECTED BY PEOPLE

3000 MILES

KING

LOWER HOUSE

ENGLAND

Sketch 15.   You will note that the heading of the sketch is "Royal Colonies." Just what does that mean? The word "royal" means pertaining to the King. The King had a lot to do with how the eight colonies were governed. That's probably why they are referred to as the "Royal Colonies." The setup was as follows . . .

Lower House . . . Elected by people
Upper House . . . Appointed by governor
Governor . . . Appointed by King

Let us keep in mind, for a proposed law to become a law it had to be okayed by both the Lower and Upper Houses. Since the Upper House members were appointed (given their jobs) by the governor and the governor was appointed (given his job) by the King, a lot of laws the people wanted and needed were blocked in the Upper House. This caused almost continuous trouble and hard feeling.

No doubt, when the representatives from these eight colonies met in Philadelphia to write our Constitution, they had a lot to say in favor of electing the people who make our laws.

CHAPTER 9

The Courts
(In The Colonies)

We have shown how the colonies were governed. We have shown
to some extent how the laws were made in most of the colonies.
As mentioned before, most people are content to obey laws. We
are taught that from the day we are born. However, it is necessary
(and fair) to have some means to take care of people who step out
of line. That's why we have courts. That's why the colonies had
courts. That brings up the question: What kind of court system did
the colonies have? Where did it come from?

That's easy to answer. Most of the people came from England.
They adopted the English system — not in every detail, but for
the most part, it was the same. But, what was it like?

It was like this. Then, as it is now, when someone was accused
of doing wrong, there had to be a trial before a judge and twelve
people (a jury). (See sketch 16) A person was innocent until proven
guilty beyond a reasonable doubt. As in England, judges used the
common law practice. But, what is *common law? Common law* is
practiced when a judge makes a decision based on the decisions
made by other judges in similar cases in the past. In other words,
if several judges in the past gave a man a few days in jail for stealing a pig, it became *common law* to give a few days in jail for pig
stealing.

It is to be noted that the judges were appointed by the governors.
Final appeals were made to the King. But, what is an appeal? An
appeal is actually a request to a person of higher authority or to
a higher court for a second judgment. Sometimes, new facts relative

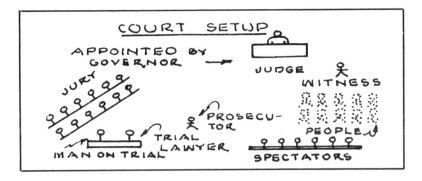

Sketch 16. This sketch gives a general idea how the court system was set up. It came from England. It is pretty much the system we use today.

On the left side of the sketch one will see "man on trial." Next to him is a "trial lawyer," who is on the side of the man on trial. He talks for him.

In the lower center part of the sketch are a number of people sitting on a bench. They are spectators. Trials are open to the public.

In the right lower part of the sketch is the prosecutor. One could say he's on the side of the people. Now, what does that mean? Well, here's the story.

As one knows, all of us are included in "the people." If a person steps out of line and does something harmful, it is logical to assume that he is an enemy of the people. The prosecutor is a lawyer who is on the people's side. He talks for the people. The dotted "stick men" above and to the right of the prosecutor represent the unseen people who the prosecutor represents.

Above "the people" one will see "the witness." He is there to tell what he knows about the case at hand. Each of the lawyers has the privilege of calling any witness in the trial.

At top left in the sketch is the judge. His job is to see that the trial is fair. Since there is a jury in this trial, the judge sets the penalty (according to law) if the man is found guilty.

The jury, shown on the left side, decides if the man is guilty.

to the case come to light, or perhaps the person who has been tried thinks that he has been treated unfairly.

Note: *Indict* means to formally charge a person with a crime (by a grand jury).

CHAPTER 10

The Gradual Change

For a period of time, as mentioned before, the people in the colonies kept to themselves. That is, they lived pretty much within their own borders and were content to do so. However, as time went on, there was a gradual change. It developed that it was good business to get acquainted with the people in the other colonies. If one fellow made shirts and needed potatoes, it was worthwhile for him to be able to deal with another fellow who raised potatoes and needed shirts.

However, there were some difficulties. For one thing, each colony had its own kind of money. A farmer in New Jersey crossing over into New York to sell his farm products had a hard time figuring what to charge. Sometimes the people of one colony would tax all the products shipped in from another colony. In time they began to see that a policy of that nature, in the long run, would hurt everyone.

In time, little by little, changes were made. People in one colony looked more kindly at the people in the other colonies. They began to see a need for things that could be accomplished only with the help of their neighbors. As an example, they began to think of some kind of protection in case they were attacked by a foreign nation. Certainly they couldn't get together much of an army on their own.

To the student:
You will note — in the above chapter the colonies are beginning to reach out to their neighboring colonies. You could say it was the beginning of "nationalism." But, what is "nationalism?" It can be

described as a feeling of loyalty (that all of us have) for the town and state we live in and yet at the same time a feeling of loyalty to our country. We are willing to let the country be the "big boss" as long as we have its respect — also, its recognition of our rights.

CHAPTER 11

Trouble With England

Along about 1763 something new was beginning to happen. The attitude of the King and Parliament changed. But, what's Parliament? It's English lawmakers.

In the past there had been some quarrels with the governors. The people had been dissatisfied in a lot of ways. However, they learned to live with it. But this, this was different. The governors began putting new demands on the colonists. But, why? Why the big change in the governors? It was money. The people of England were hurting for money. They had just finished seven years of war. They were in debt. An era of expansion was in progress. Always, that sort of thing takes money. What better place to get it than the colonies? England owned the colonies. Why shouldn't they help?

The King and Parliament figured out various ways to tax the people in the colonies. The governors had to do the collecting. The patriots, of course, vented their anger on the governors who, in turn, took the word to the King. And, of course, the King retaliated by taxing heavier and heavier.

The English became very demanding as to whom the colonists sold their products. For example, if the English people needed potatoes, then they demanded that the colonists ship them potatoes. The people in the colonies had no one in England to take part in deciding who could be taxed and by how much.

Of course, the people strongly resented the treatment they were getting from England. They felt hurt. The feeling was catching on. People talked. Word got around. It was sort of in the air. People

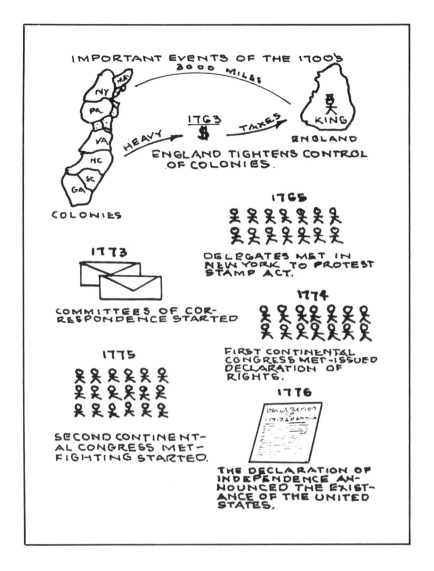

were thinking, "We're being pushed around; something has to be done." People in some of the colonies started to correspond with people in other colonies. It became apparent that the colonists were not going to take this treatment sitting down.

CHAPTER 12

The Beginning

It was evident the people in the colonies needed two things:
1. to pull away from England, and
2. to form a national government.
The process of getting anything done developed slowly. There was no organization and few leaders. It took time, but things did occur from time to time that you could say pushed them in the direction in which they wanted to go.

As is usually the case, when people feel that they have been treated badly, they get together and talk it over. That's what happened. In 1765 delegates from nine colonies met in New York[1] to discuss their difficulties. During the next few years Committees of Correspondence were formed in each of the colonies. Word was getting around.

The people in the colonies liked tea and drank lots of it. The King said, in effect, "We need money; they drink tea; we'll put a stiff tax on it." This so angered the patriots in Boston that they dumped several chests of tea in the sea. In response to this act, Parliament designed and passed several laws to punish the colonists.

In 1774 delegates from nearly all the colonies met in Philadelphia[2] and issued a "paper"[3] that protested how they had been treated

---

[1]This meeting was called "The Stamp Act Congress." The English used stamps as a means of collecting taxes. This system became known as "The Stamp Act."

[2]This meeting was called "The First Continental Congress."

[3]This paper was called "The Declaration of Rights."

by the English. Also they sent word back to the people to boycott English goods.

Nearly two years later the colonies again met in Philadelphia[4]. This was an important meeting. In April 1775 fighting had broken out between the patriots and the British. No doubt the fighting prompted the colonists to assume the responsibility necessary to run the affairs of a nation. Actually, for the next six years, the delegates who made up this meeting handled the business of this would-be nation. Here are some things they accomplished:

...organized an army,

...appointed George Washington as its commander,

...took steps to borrow money and issue currency,

...negotiated with foreign nations,

...edited and wrote the Declaration of Independence on July 4, 1776,

...urged each state to form new governments.

Definitions:

The word *congress* means a meeting together of persons.

The word *continental* means pertaining to one of the large divisions of unbroken land.

The word *declaration* means a statement.

The word *independent* means not subject to control of others.

The Declaration of Independence is a statement (written by Thomas Jefferson and okayed by the second Continental Congress) that says the 13 colonies are free and independent of Great Britain.

---

[4]This meeting was called "The Second Continental Congress."

CHAPTER 13

State Government

When the fighting started, many officials returned to England. That left most of the colonies in need of new state governments. (See sketch 17)

The lawmakers at the Second Continental Congress meeting in Philadelphia sent word to the colonies to establish new state governments. It did not take them long to get started. No doubt they were glad to be rid of the English influence, or you could say English pressure, that had developed in the last few years.

A lot of the things that make up a government were already in place.

Each state had a constitution. There were three groups of people as follows...

Executive...This was the governor (and helpers). Their job was to see that the laws were obeyed and to tend to the business affairs of the state. The governor was elected by the people.

Legislative...These were two groups of people who made laws. One was called *the upper house*. The other was called *the lower house*. Each member of the two groups was elected by the people.

Judicial...This pertains to courts of law.

THE 3 BRANCHES
STATE GOVERNMENT

UPPER HOUSE
LAWMAKERS
ELECTED
BY
PEOPLE
LEGISLATIVE
BRANCH

LOWER HOUSE
LAWMAKERS
ELECTED
BY
PEOPLE

GOVERNOR & HELPERS
BUSINESS AFFAIRS
ENFORCES LAWS
ELECTED BY PEOPLE
EXECUTIVE
BRANCH

COURTS
JUD.
WIT.
JURY
LAWYER
PROS.
DEFEND   SPECTATORS
JUSTICE OF THE PEACE
COUNTY COURTS
COURT OF APPEALS
JUDICIAL
BRANCH

Sketch 17.   When the thirteen colonies became states, what it took
to be governed was pretty much in place.

CHAPTER 14

Being Part
Of A Nation

Since each of the states was forming a government to its own satisfaction, it brought up something for them to think about. This was a national government. Most of us like to run our own business with no strings attached. So, it was with the states. Each had its own government confined to its own borders. However, it's somewhat like a young man who reaches his sixteenth birthday. He's a man now, big and strong. He doesn't need anyone to tell him what to do. He's old enough to make his own decisions. But, there comes a time — he needs a little help; he's in a tight spot. To whom should he go? He begins to have second thoughts. Each state, during this transition period, in its own way, was having second thoughts.

As an example, what about Virginia? What about that long coastline? Suppose a foreign nation took a notion to unload an army there and take some of the things they needed?

One state could not very well build cross-country roads, yet roads are needed to get products to market.

It takes more money than any one state could afford to build a navy.

What about disputes over boundary lines between the states?

What about tariffs? It can get into difficulties.

Of course, the need for a central government was obvious and its benefits almost endless. However, the states had recently shed themselves of one type of dictator — the King's governors. They, of course, were reluctant to put themselves in a similar position with a central government. Once in power, a central government could become careless. It could become money hungry and overtax. Things of that nature entered the minds of the people.

We will see the results of this thinking as we follow their progress toward a workable constitution.

CHAPTER 15

Writing The Rules To Be Governed By

At this time, representatives from all the states were in session in Philadelphia. They were handling the affairs of the thirteen states. They were having difficulties. They were not organized. You could say they were trying to operate without a plan. They needed a guide — a written guide. When there was a question about procedure, about who was in charge of what, they needed a rule book.

Consequently, they appointed a committee to write a set of rules by which the country would be run. (See sketch 18) Close to five years passed before the rules[1] were written and put into operation.

The committee that wrote the rules — Articles of Confederation — put in a lot of hard work. However, it simply did not work out. This congress was given the power to make laws but no way to enforce them.

The states were like a bunch of kids without a mother. They quarreled with each other. Financial troubles developed, and Congress could do little to help. They had no money. The states were expected to contribute money to run the central government, but there was no way to force them to do so.

Definitions:
The word *article* means part of a document.
The word *confederation* means the act of binding.

---

[1]Articles of Confederation

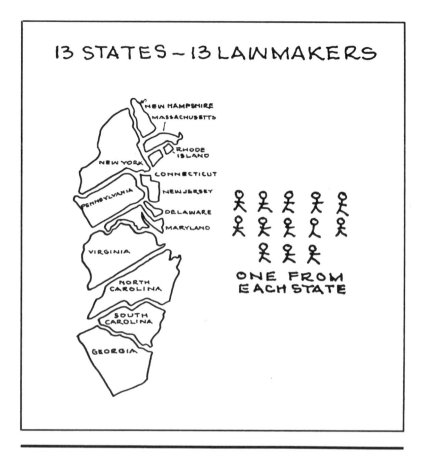

Sketch 18.   You will note from the above sketch that the setup was quite simple. Thirteen people, one from each state, made the rules. This group was called "the Congress."

Each state had one vote.

For a bill to pass, nine states had to agree.

You will note from the sketch, there is no central authority (like a president). There simply had to be some central power that could say, "Your representatives voted for this and this is the way it's going to be," and make it stick.

Definition:

The word *"congress"* means a meeting together of persons.

CHAPTER 16

The Constitutional Convention

Somewhere around the middle of the 1780s, conditions were almost to a breaking point with money problems, boundary disputes and the like. Some of the leading men in the states argued that there was an urgent need for a stronger central government that could force the states to obey the laws.

With conditions as they were, it was difficult to get anything underway. The Philadelphia group (Congress) finally suggested that the states get a convention underway to once again try to write a workable set of rules for the country. The result was the start of the constitutional convention on May 25, 1787. It took four months to get the job done. Fifty-five men worked on it. George Washington was chairman. Meetings were secret (information about them came from a diary of one of the members). Nine states had to agree before it became law.

Now, what were the people like who put this famous document together? There were farmers, lawyers, merchants, doctors, soldiers and educators. Were they old or young? Some were in their 20s; one was 81.

By Sept. 18, the job was done.

Most of us go through life living by the Constitution's rules but never have occasion to study, or, for that matter, to even read what's in it. Well, maybe some read a little bit in school. However, when the contents of the Constitution are mentioned, one part that is just sure to be talked about is the Preamble. (See sketch 18A) For that reason it is worthwhile to study.

PREAMBLE

*"We, the people of the United States, in order
to form a more perfect union, establish justice,
insure domestic tranquility, provide for the common
defense, promote the general welfare, and secure
the blessings of liberty to ourselves and our
posterity, do ordain and establish this Constitution
for the United States of America."*

Sketch 18A. *Explanation:*

IN ORDER TO FORM A MORE PERFECT UNION
The word "union" mentioned above refers to all of the states combined. A "more perfect union" refers to each state getting along well with the other states.

ESTABLISH JUSTICE
That means that there shall be no unfair trials or punishments. In other words, our courts shall be run by the people.

INSURE DOMESTIC TRANQUILITY
The word "domestic" in this case refers to the states as they were members of a family. Our national courts are designed to settle quarrels between the states. "Tranquil" means undisturbed.

PROVIDE FOR THE COMMON DEFENSE
The Constitution permits our government to keep an army and navy to protect us from foreign attack.

TO PROMOTE GENERAL WELFARE
That means that the national government is to promote health, happiness and prosperity of the people.

BILL OF RIGHTS

THE BILL OF RIGHTS SAYS —

1 YOU CAN WORSHIP, SAY AND PRINT WHAT
   YOU PLEASE AND TELL THE GOVERNMENT
   WHAT YOU DISLIKE.
2 YOU ARE ALLOWED TO USE AND OWN
   WEAPONS FOR LAWFUL PURPOSES.
3 SOLDIERS CANNOT STAY IN YOUR HOME
   AGAINST YOUR WISHES.
4 WITH OUT A WARRANT NO FEDERAL OF-
   FICER CAN ARREST YOU.
5 A GRAND JURY MUST DECIDE IF YOU ARE
   TO BE TRIED FOR A SERIOUS CRIME. YOU
   CANNOT BE TRIED TWICE FOR THE SAME
   CRIME. YOU CANNOT BE FORCED TO SAY
   ANYTHING AGAINST YOURSELF. THE GOV-
   ERNMENT CANNOT TAKE YOUR PROPER-
   TY WITHOUT PAYING FOR IT.
6 IF ACCUSED OF A FEDERAL CRIME, YOU
   MUST HAVE A FAIR TRIAL.
7 ALL CIVIL CASES (EXCEPT SMALL) MUST
   HAVE A JURY TRIAL.
8 THERE WILL BE NO CRUEL OR UNUSUAL
   PUNISHMENTS.
9 ALL FEDERAL RIGHTS ARE LISTED IN
   THE CONSTITUTION.
10 RIGHTS NOT LISTED IN THE CONSTITUTION
   GO TO THE PEOPLE.

Sketch 18B. Definitions:

Grand jury...A body of 12 to 23 people that investigates accusa-
tions against people.

Civil law...Pertains to the rights of individuals and legal actions
involving them.

Criminal Law...Pertains to the conduct of individuals. The government is always the prosecutor since the crimes are
against the public.

Habeas Corpus...is an order stating that a prisoner be brought to
court to determine if he can legally be held.

Warrant...A statement on paper that justifies an arrest.

First, the meaning of the word. Preamble is the introduction to a story. Actually, it is a long sentence at the beginning of the Constitution stating why the Constitution is written.

Another part of the Constitution that is often mentioned is the Bill of Rights. (See sketch 18B) Here's the story.

It is to be remembered that writing the Constitution was one thing. Getting it signed into law was another. Some of the states held out. They were afraid that some people, when they came to power, would take advantage of the people under them. The result was the addition of ten amendments to the Constitution that guaranteed the freedom of both the states and individuals from abuses of power by the national government. These ten amendments became known as the Bill of Rights. Enough of the states signed up for the Constitution to become law.

Amending the Constitution

As mentioned before, the Constitution can be amended. At first thought one would think that the lawmakers would get together, make a few speeches, then vote and that would just about be it. Not so. It's not that simple. Here's the way it is:

Any member of the Congress can suggest an amendment. Then it has to be determined if the suggested amendment is worthy of consideration. This can be done by two methods, as follows:

(a) by a two-thirds majority vote of the House of Representatives and the Senate.

(b) by a national constitutional convention with all states represented.

If, by one of the above-mentioned methods, the suggested amendment is deemed worthy of consideration, it can be made part of the Constitution by the approval of...

(a) Lawmakers in three-fourths of the states, or

(b) three-fourths of the states at each state's convention. (See sketch 18C)

Now, the next thing that comes to mind is why the Constitution ever has to be changed. It's a good list of rules. It works. Why change it? Here's why. Time has changed the way we live. As the way we live changes, it sometimes is an advantage to change the rules by which we live. Some things that time has changed are as follows:

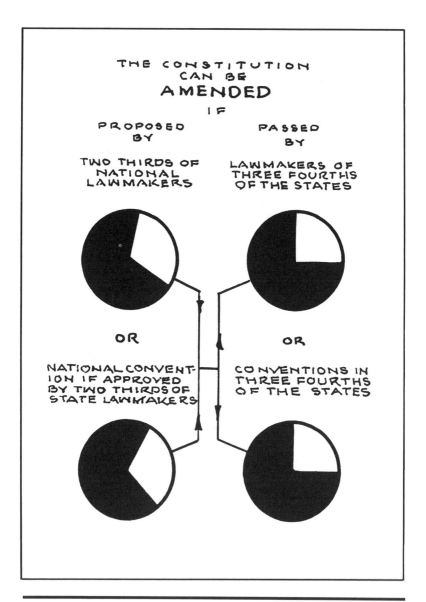

Sketch 18C.   As shown above, our Constitution can be changed only by the state and federal governments working together.

We have the same amount of land, but many more people to feed. We used to travel by horse, now it's by air. We used to figure with a pencil, now it's a computer.

A question. Why was the method of amending the Constitution made so difficult? Here's why. It was because foolish or dangerous changes are not likely to be accepted. The people must think carefully about every change that is suggested. However, let us keep in mind that changes can be made.

CHAPTER 17

The
Three Branches

We have been reviewing the events that gave the colonists the know-how to write our Constitution. We are now beginning to study how our government works.

The first thing to keep in mind is that our government is simply groups of people with jobs to do. If we can get in mind what their duties are and can identify each group with the more than one name that it goes by, we are well on our way to understanding how our government works.

Our government is made up of three departments. Some people speak of them as three branches. They are called three departments (or branches) because the jobs they do are of a different nature. They are as follows:

Executive branch
The President (and helpers)
> His job is to see that the laws are obeyed. He tends to the nation's business. He's the big boss. If our country was a corporation, he would be the general manager.

Legislative Branch
Senate (Upper House)
House of Representatives (Lower House)
> Their jobs are to make laws.

Judicial Branch
The Supreme Court
> Their job is (when called upon) to interpret the meaning of the Constitution and to decide what's fair. (See sketch 19)

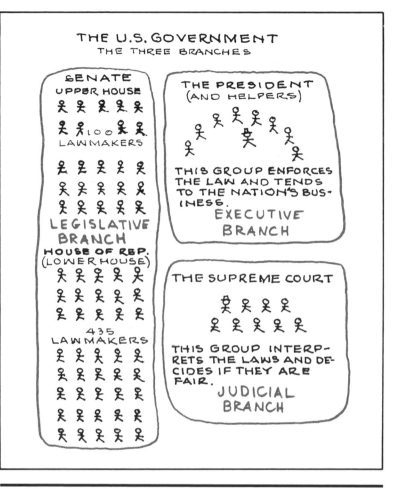

Sketch 19.   This sketch shows an outline of what our government is composed of. It is well to keep in mind where it came from.

Definitions:
  Executive is a manager of public affairs.
  Legislative has power to make laws.
  Judicial pertains to the courts of law and judges
  Interpret explains meaning.

CHAPTER 18

Too Many Names

Different words are often used to refer to the same thing. For example, the House of Representatives can be referred to as the Lower House or just the House or the lawmakers.

Then, too, to make the subject more confusing, the Senate can be referred to as the Upper Body.

We can't do anything about how names are used, but we can familiarize ourselves with all of the names. We can then know to which group the text or teacher is referring. (See sketches 19A & 19B)

To the student: It is common practice for the beginner to find it very confusing and difficult to get in mind what some names mean.

The time it takes to get the four groups on page 49 well in mind would be well spent. They are the basis of American government.

It is to be noted that writers of articles in the newspapers and magazines use names of groups to tell about what goes on in Washington. Obviously, a writer is not going to say *House of Representatives* when he can say House. Or to give another example, he is not going to say *Senate and House of Representatives* when he can say Congress and so on.

Once the meaning of the names is learned, political writings can be viewed differently and enjoyed.

As indicated in Sketch 19A, names are of little value without an understanding of the importance of the groups to which they refer.

AMERICAN GOVERNMENT
WITH OUT NAMES

100 PEOPLE
100 PEOPLE WHO MAKE LAWS

435 PEOPLE
435 PEOPLE WHO MAKE LAWS

1 PERSON WITH HELPERS
OUR PRESIDENT ENFORCES THE LAWS

9 PEOPLE
9 PEOPLE DECIDE WHAT'S FAIR

Sketch 19A.   You will note from the above sketch that when the parts of our government are not named, the basic setup is quite simple. Actually it's simply four groups of people, each group with its own job to do.

AMERICAN GOVERNMENT
(WITH NAMES)

SENATE
UPPER HOUSE
UPPER BODY
LAWMAKERS

100 PEOPLE

CONGRESS
LEGISLATURE
LEGISLATIVE BRANCH
LAWMAKERS
THE 2 HOUSES

435 PEOPLE

HOUSE OF REPRESENTATIVES
THE HOUSE
THE LOWER HOUSE
LAWMAKERS
THE LOWER BODY

1 PERSON
WITH HELPERS

THE PRESIDENT
EXECUTIVE BRANCH
THE WHITE HOUSE

9 PEOPLE

THE SUPREME COURT
JUDICIAL BRANCH
FEDERAL COURT
THE HIGHEST COURT

Sketch 19B.   On the left we have shown the four groups of people that compose our American government. To the right of each group we have listed the various names used to refer to each group.

You will note the top group is composed of 100 people. It's name is the *Senate*. It is often called the upper house, the upper body or lawmakers.

Under the Senate you will note a group of 435 people. Its name is the *House of Representatives*. It is often called the House, the lower house, lawmakers or the lower body.

Since the above-mentioned groups of 100 and 435 people are lawmakers, they are often referred to under one name called *the Congress*. They are often called the Legislature, the legislative branch, lawmakers or the two houses.

The next group is *the President* and his helpers. All of us are acquainted with his job and, of course, know his name. Other than the President, his area is often called the executive branch or the White House.

The bottom group is composed of nine people. Its name is *the Supreme Court*. It is often referred to as the judicial branch, the federal court or the high court.

As we have shown, 21 names can be applied to one of the groups of people. The sketch was drawn to help us picture in our minds just which group any one of the names refers to when we see it in print or hear it mentioned. We need to be as familiar with what any of the names represent as we are when we hear the word "chair" or "bed" mentioned.

CHAPTER 19

Separation
Of Powers

If two men entered the grocery business as partners, it is obvious that for the business to be successful they would have to make a decision relative to their duties. For example, they would sign an agreement that one would be responsible for the book work — ordering, pricing, bill paying — and the other partner would have charge of the sales end of the business — the clerks, displays and so on.

Such an arrangement could be successful because the men want it to succeed. Then, too, they can refer to the written agreement if anything comes up.

There is pretty much the same arrangement in our government. Our Constitution tells us that:

. . . Congress is to make the laws.

. . . The President is to enforce the laws.

. . . The Supreme Court is to decide if the laws are fair.

In other words, each branch of the government is to stick to its job. The President cannot pass a law, the Congress cannot enforce the law and only the Supreme Court (when asked) can judge if the laws are fair. In other words, no branch has complete control. Of course, a give-and-take attitude has to exist if anything is to be accomplished.

All of the above is called "separation of powers." (See sketch 19C)

The term itself is somewhat confusing: Separation of powers really means separation of jobs. It is important to know why people doing these various jobs should not be together.

SEPARATION OF POWERS

LEGISLATIVE BRANCH
THEY MAKE THE LAWS

HOUSE   SENATE

435   100
LAWMAKERS   LAWMAKERS

EXECUTIVE BRANCH
THEY ENFORCE
THE LAWS
                               JUDICIAL BRANCH
                               THEY DECIDE
                               WHAT'S FAIR

THE PRESIDENT   SUPREME COURT
(AND HELPERS)

Sketch 19C. This sketch is to help us get in mind what *separation of powers* means.

Now comes the big question. Why are the three branches of our government placed in separate groups? Here's why. The members of each of the three branches are selected by different procedures and are pretty much independent of each other. All of which serves to keep the members from doing unjust and unwise things. It keeps them attached to the jobs they were assigned to do.

When a government, or any part of it, becomes too powerful, there is a tendency for it to take away the people's rights.

CHAPTER 20

Checks
And Balances

Checks and balances has to do with the three branches of our government.
The President,
The lawmakers,
The Supreme Court.
The duties of each of the above-mentioned branches enable each branch to check the power of the other two branches. It is called *checks and balances*.

Perhaps some examples will give a better understanding. To become a law, each bill has to be signed by the President. If the President doesn't like the bill, he can return it to the lawmakers unsigned (vetoed). Then, in turn, Congress can again vote on the bill and, with enough votes, can pass it.

In a related manner, the President can give an executive order for something very important to him. If the lawmakers don't like his proposal, they can refuse to appropriate the money needed for his project.

Another check: the President appoints the Supreme Court members, but his appointments must be okayed by the Senate.

Another check that comes into play every year is in the establishment of the federal budget. First, let's be sure we understand what a budget is. You could say a budget is two plans (which we will call "a" and "b") written on a piece of paper.

Plan "a" is a list showing money expected to come in.
Plan "b" is a list showing money expected to be paid out.

The federal budget is the above-mentioned plans ("a" and "b") that are put together by the President and helpers. However, what the President has planned has to be approved by the two groups of lawmakers. Committees are formed by each group to study the President's lists. Finally, Congress has to find the money to pay for the things that the President has listed. It often works into quite a controversy. It is an annual event that starts every January.

Another great check that should be remembered is the voter. You can bet on it; the office holder keeps in mind that he can be voted out in the next election.

Now, we have explained above what the system of checks and balances is. (See sketch 19D) But, why do we have it? Here's why. Sometimes when people are elected to office, they seem to forget that their job is to serve the people. Consequently, they pass laws and make appointments that benefit themselves, or perhaps only a small group of the people. For example, they could appoint an unqualified relative or friend to a high-paying job. The system of checks and balances makes it difficult for this to happen. In this case, the voters could vote them out of office for favoring relatives.

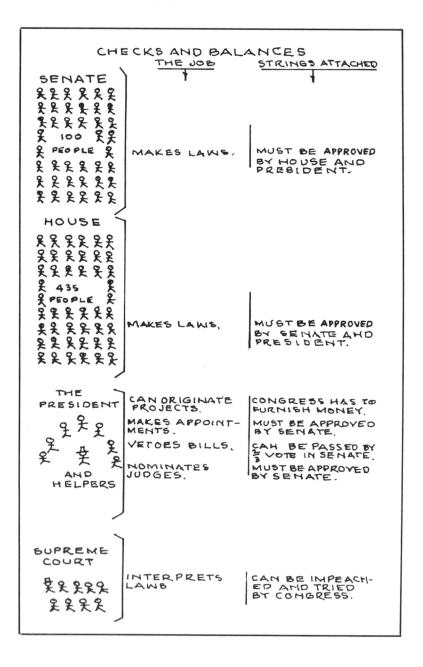

CHECKS AND BALANCES

THE JOB   STRINGS ATTACHED

SENATE

100 PEOPLE

MAKES LAWS.   MUST BE APPROVED
                      BY HOUSE AND
                      PRESIDENT.

HOUSE

435 PEOPLE

MAKES LAWS,   MUST BE APPROVED
                      BY SENATE AND
                      PRESIDENT.

THE PRESIDENT

AND HELPERS

CAN ORIGINATE   CONGRESS HAS TO
PROJECTS.   FURNISH MONEY.

MAKES APPOINT-   MUST BE APPROVED
MENTS.   BY SENATE.

VETOES BILLS.   CAN BE PASSED BY
                      ⅔ VOTE IN SENATE.

NOMINATES   MUST BE APPROVED
JUDGES.   BY SENATE.

SUPREME COURT

INTERPRETS   CAN BE IMPEACH-
LAWS   ED AND TRIED
                      BY CONGRESS.

Sketch 19D.   All of us know what is meant when we hear someone say an agreement was reached but there were strings attached. Well, that gives us a good way of explaining the method that is used to prevent too much power from being concentrated in one person or one group of people.

Strings were attached to many of the projects that the people of the three branches (of our government) were assigned to.

You will note in the sketch at left are the branches, at center are the projects (jobs they were assigned to) and at right are the attached strings.

CHAPTER 21

What Is Meant By "The Party"

Up to now we have said little about political parties. They are hard to understand by reading a book. Most people, after a lot of living and a lot of newspaper reading, form some kind of an opinion. However, if you asked the average person what our political system is, he probably would say, "Democrats and Republicans." And, if you questioned him further and said, "What's that?", he would no doubt say, "Well, let's see now...that's two parties."

Since that is what our system is, we will begin by telling what a party is. A party is a number of people grouped together under one name. Some people think of a party as a group of people that thinks of things in the same way. However, you can't find any two Democrats or Republicans who will give you the same reasons why they are listed with either party.

The dictionary says that a Democrat is "one who adheres to democracy." It says a Republican is "one who belongs to the Republican Party." Not much help.

Perhaps there is something in all of us that "just belonging" gives us a sense of security.

Generally, there does seem to be a tendency of the better educated and monied people to hover under the Republican banner. While on the other hand, the Democrats are composed mostly of working people.

From the above description of what a party is, one could get the impression that political parties are not important. Not so. They are very important. Here's why. Just about everything is decided by votes. Whether to improve the streets of your hometown, elect a governor or decide who will be the next president, the most votes make the decision.

It so happens that we have only two parties.[1] So, if you vote, you "go" either Democratic or Republican.

Now, the Democratic Party has an organization all of its own. The Republican Party has an organization all of its own.

If we understand the workings of the above-mentioned parties, we are making considerable progress toward understanding our political system. That's why we will be talking about Democrats and Republicans in the next few pages.

Politics

The definition of some words is as confusing as the word. One such word is "politics." You hear someone say, "That's politics for you" or, "He's into politics" or, "That's a political situation."

So, we wonder. . . what is the meaning? Most of us say, "Well now, I'll look it up in the dictionary." That works out fine for some words, but not for politics. Here's why. The dictionary says that politics is "the art of government." But, what's that? We're no better off than we were. Well, we could ask a teacher who knows but could only give us a dictionary definition. Here's why. Defining politics is almost impossible. It's like trying to define the taste of apples. Or, perhaps trying to tell a 6-year-old what puppy-love is. After we have studied government for a while and after we have read in the newspapers about the goings-on in Washington, we have our own definition of politics.

'**To the student:** The objective of the above chapter is to remind all of us that it's common to be a little slow to grasp the meaning of some words and definitions found in the study of government.

---

[1]There is no law that says there can't be more than two political parties. Parties other than the Democrats and Republicans make their appearance from time to time. However, they seldom attract enough followers to amount to anything.

CHAPTER 22

State
Political Structure

First, just what is meant by "state political structure"? Well, you could say the word "political" has to do with governing. You could say the word "structure" has to do with building. So, it is fair to say "political structure" has to do with how the art of governing is put together.

There is a Democratic Party in each state. There is a Republican Party in each state. Since there are fifty states, that means there are one hundred state political parties. However, the structure of each is pretty much the same.

From hearing people talk and reading the newspapers, we are sometimes led to think that officeholders are elected in the state capital or maybe in Washington. Not so. It takes place right in your own neighborhood — in the precinct. (See sketch 20) Now, what's a "precinct"? It's an area that's outlined so people will know where to go to vote. It's convenient.

To be able to vote, one has to be registered. But what's that? It really means that a person is enrolled at the proper place, which, in turn, entitles him to vote. It helps officials keep track of people, where they live and if they are entitled to vote. In the farming areas, there are sometimes less than one hundred voters in a precinct. In a heavily populated area, there could be perhaps two thousand voters in one precinct. There is a precinct leader for each party. His job is to keep the voters lined up to vote for his party.

We see so much in the paper about the goings-on in Washington,

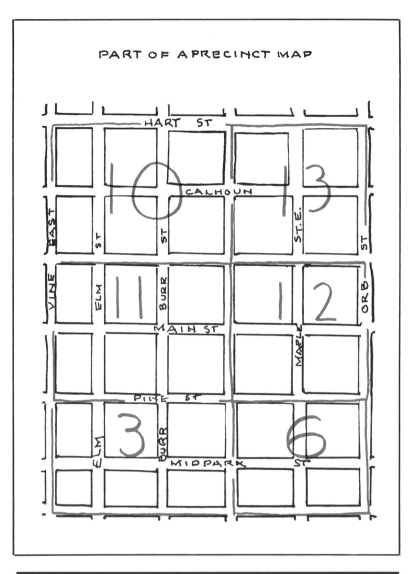

Sketch 20.   A precinct is an area containing a place to vote and the living quarters of the people who are to vote there. In other words, it's lines on a map that tell you where to vote.

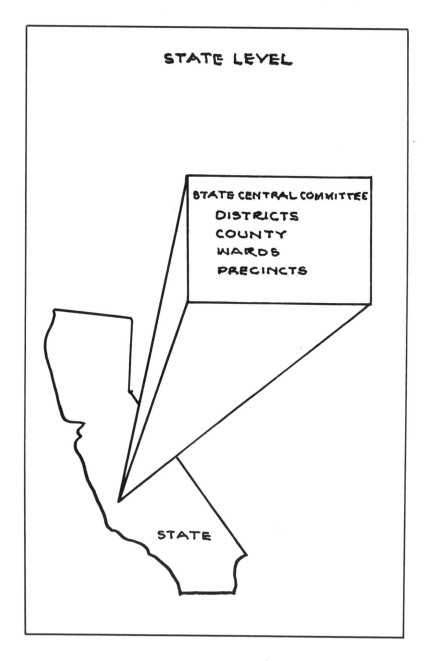

the state capitals and the like, we have a tendency to underrate the importance of what takes place at the precinct level. Actually, what takes place in the precinct is the guts of the election process. It is the beginning. You can think of what takes place as being likened to the relationship of three people. There is the voter; on one side of him is a Democrat pulling at him to vote Democratic. On the other side of him is a Republican pulling at him to vote Republican. Now, it is the decision that this voter makes when he is all alone in the booth that determines who winds up in the state capital or in Washington.

In some of the larger cities several of the precincts are grouped together to form a *ward* organization. Ward committees are formed. They direct the political activity of the ward. They plan parties and programs.

County organizations are made up of committees that are responsible for party affairs of various kinds. There is usually a chairman who is elected by the committee members. He often has considerable power. He selects candidates for office and has some control over government jobs.

In the state structure there are several district committees formed. They handle party business in districts established for the election of congressmen. Similar districts are formed for state lawmakers.

The State Central Committee is at the top of each state party structure. You could say it directs the party activity of the state. However, it has no direct authority over any of the lower levels. State Central Committees are composed of members of congressional districts, state legislative districts or counties. They are responsible for carrying out the policies of the party. (See sketches 21 & 22)

Dictionary definition:
    A *district* is a defined tract of land.

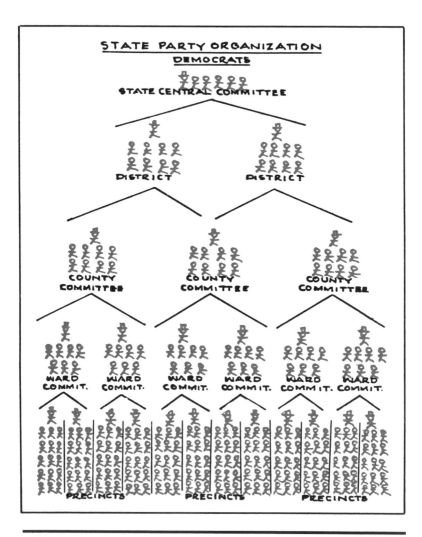

Sketch 21.   Each state has an organization of Democrats. Now, a
question: what's it for? It's to get Democrats elected.
    They are all pretty much alike. The above sketch gives an idea of
the setup.

Note: The number of people in the precincts or in the committees
varies.

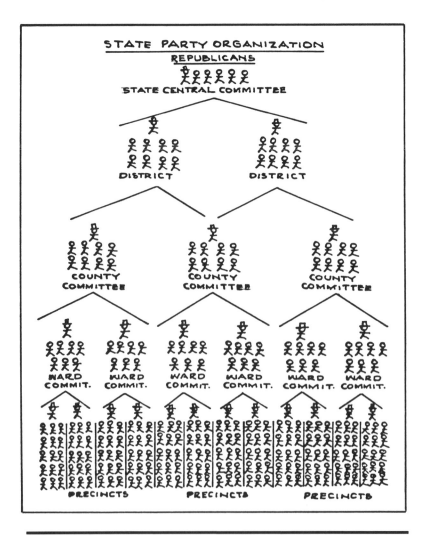

Sketch 22. Each state has an organization of Republicans. Now, a question: What's it for? It's to get Republicans elected.

They are all pretty much alike. The above sketch gives an idea of the setup.

Note: The number of people in the precincts or in the committees varies.

CHAPTER 23

The
Executive Branch

The President is the part of the United States government that we hear the most about. We see him on television the most. He is the big boss. He points the way. He sets the stage to deal with the nation's biggest problems. When necessary, he sees to it that laws are made to deal with these problems. He sees that the laws are obeyed. He is elected to office. (See sketch 23)

To Be In the Running

One of the first things that enters the mind is, What does a person have to do or be to get presidential votes?

One thing that helps is to have money. You can't work from nine to five making a living and have enough time left to run around over the country telling people you are the man for the job. Another is to have the right personality. You can't describe what it is, but some people have it and some don't.

He can't be too chummy, but on the other hand he can't be aloof. In other words, he has to have balance.

If he has held office in another capacity, like the governor of a state (most especially if his tenure has been in a prosperous time), it gives him a better chance.

And, above most other requirements he has to look like a President. He does not necessarily have to be handsome, but it is best not to look too ordinary. People like to be proud of what their President looks like.

Of course, a good education is mandatory, along with the ability

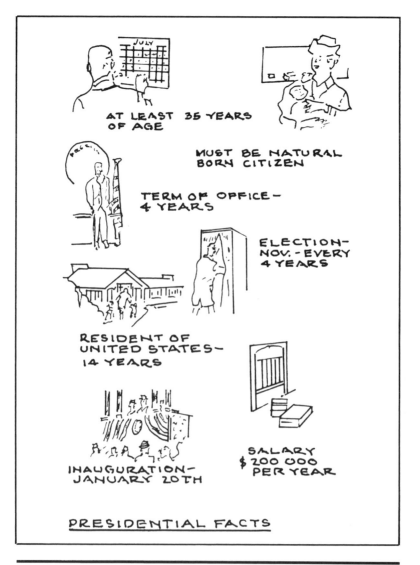

AT LEAST 35 YEARS OF AGE

MUST BE NATURAL BORN CITIZEN

TERM OF OFFICE – 4 YEARS

ELECTION – NOV. - EVERY 4 YEARS

RESIDENT OF UNITED STATES – 14 YEARS

INAUGURATION – JANUARY 20TH

SALARY $200 000 PER YEAR

PRESIDENTIAL FACTS

Sketch 23.   The President must be: a natural-born citizen, at least 35 years of age, resident of the United States 14 years.

Term of office — four years, Inauguration — January 20th, Election — November every fourth year, Salary — $200,000 per year.

to make a good speech. A candidate can get some college professor to write his speeches, but no one can deliver them for him.

More Requirements

Now, the problem at hand is to learn at least a few things (other than good looks and being the right age) that can push a person along toward the big job.

One thing, he just about has to be either a Democrat or a Republican. Well, he could be something else, say an Independent. However, there would have to be very unusual conditions, because the people who do the voting are mostly either Democrats or Republicans.

One thing is sure. To be a serious candidate, a person has to have the backing of a good-sized group of people. One way to do this is to get nominated by a national nominating committee at one of the party conventions.

Another way is for the candidate to get his name entered in a primary. But, what's a primary? A primary is an election in which the voters select a candidate to run under the party's banner. In other words, the primary election is used to choose the candidates, then the general election is used to choose the officeholder. Many states hold primary elections. A candidate can get a pretty good idea how he stands with voters by putting his name on the ballot.

The President's Job

Most of us have never seen our President. Well, we do see his picture on television. We've heard him talk. But the fact remains, we have not seen him at work. What does he do? We pay him about two hundred thousand dollars per year. What does he give us in return?

He gives us management. That's just about it. Our government has been in operation for quite a long time. Throughout the years, it has become divided into departments. When the President comes into office, the departments are in operation. His job is to pick the right person to run each department. These people comprise the Cabinet. (See sketch 24)

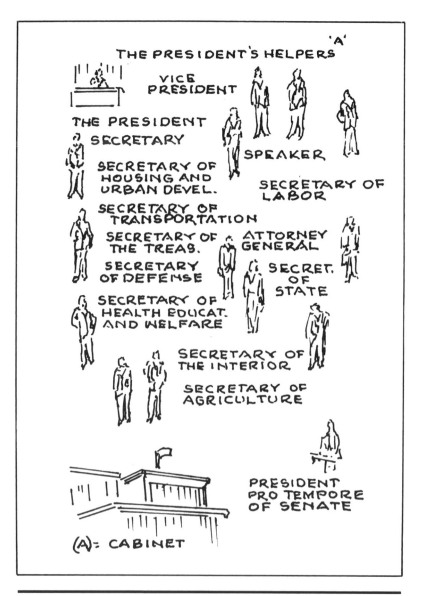

THE PRESIDENT'S HELPERS · A ·

VICE PRESIDENT

THE PRESIDENT

SECRETARY

SPEAKER

SECRETARY OF HOUSING AND URBAN DEVEL.

SECRETARY OF LABOR

SECRETARY OF TRANSPORTATION

SECRETARY OF THE TREAS.

ATTORNEY GENERAL

SECRETARY OF DEFENSE

SECRET. OF STATE

SECRETARY OF HEALTH EDUCAT. AND WELFARE

SECRETARY OF THE INTERIOR

SECRETARY OF AGRICULTURE

PRESIDENT PRO TEMPORE OF SENATE

(A) = CABINET

Sketch 24.   It is the President's responsibility to choose the right person for each job.

CHAPTER 24

The
Electoral College

The way a President is elected is somewhat confusing. You would think that everyone would go to the voting place, put a mark by someone's name, then some official would count the marks, and that would just about be it. Not so. It's not that simple. You could say that several people from each state meet at the state capital and vote. The vote decides who is elected. Those people are spoken of as the Electoral College. But, what's the meaning of the term? Electoral refers to electing. College means several people. So, Electoral College means several people who vote.

Each state is entitled to as many electors as there are senators and representatives from that state in Congress. State electors are expected to vote for the party that chose them. However, only a few states legally require their electors to vote for the winning candidate.

To be elected, the President and Vice President must receive a majority of the electoral votes. (Majority means more than half.) If a majority of electoral votes is not received by a presidential candidate, then the election is decided by a majority vote of the House of Representatives, each state having one vote. The Senate, by majority vote, will decide the Vice President if no candidate received a majority of the electoral votes. (See sketches 25 & 26)

Note: Sometimes the electors are not listed on the ballot on which the presidential nominee is listed. Consequently, many people do not realize that they are, when they vote for the President, at

HOW A PRESIDENT IS ELECTED

IN THE SUMMER OF AN ELECTION YEAR—

THE DEMOCRATS AT A STATE CONVENTION NOMINATE SEVERAL ELECTORS.	THE REPUBLICANS AT A STATE CONVENTION NOMINATE SEVERAL ELECTORS.

1
THEN IN NOVEMBER THE PEOPLE VOTE FOR THE ELECTORS AS THEY VOTE FOR THE PRESIDENT.

2
THEN IN DECEMBER - THE ELECTORS (BELONGING TO THE PARTY THAT RECEIVED THE MOST VOTES) PROCEED TO THEIR RESPECTIVE STATE CAPITAL AND CAST THEIR VOTE FOR THE WINNER.

3
THEN IN A FEW DAYS THE RESULTS ARE SENT TO WASHINGTON.

4
ON JAN. 6 THE ELECTORAL VOTES ARE COUNTED IN CONGRESS WITH THE PRESIDENT OF THE SENATE PRESIDING AND DECLARING THE RESULTS OF THE ELECTION.

Sketch 25.   Each state is entitled to as many electors as there are senators and representatives from that state in Congress. State electors are expected to vote for the party that chose them. However, only a few states legally require their electors to vote for the winning candidate.

To be elected, the President and Vice President must receive a majority of the electoral votes. (Note: Majority means more than half.) If a majority of votes is not received by a presidential candidate, then the election is decided by a majority vote of the House of Representatives with each state having one vote. The Senate, by majority vote, will decide the Vice President if no candidate received a majority of the electoral votes.

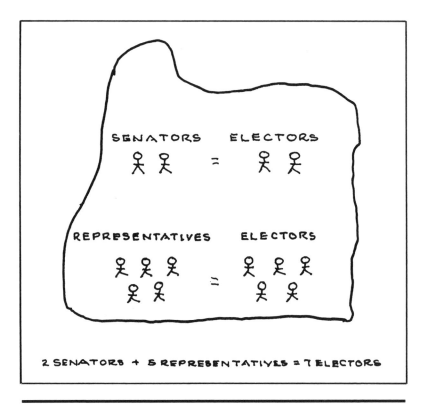

Sketch 26. Question: How many electoral votes is each state entitled to?
Answer: The sum of the number of its members in the House of Representatives and in the Senate.

the same time voting for the electors.

You could say our laws are such that we can't elect a President of the United States. However, we can (and do) every fourth year elect a group of people (called the Electoral College) from each state that meets in each state capital, and they elect our President.

Definitions:

"Grass roots" means close to, or from, the people.

"Democracy" means a government by the people, for the people.

Sketch 26A. The number of electoral votes each state receives relative to the 1980 decennial census is shown.

CHAPTER 25

Steps Toward Electing A President

There are a lot of people in our country. You could say it's a big organization. Someone has to be the boss. Someone has to be the head man. We call him our President.

Our system of government is such that the President gets his job because a majority of the people selected him. In other words, more people vote for him than any other person in an election.

Through many years of practice, it has developed that in order for a candidate to have a chance, he has to be either a Democrat or a Republican. This brings up a question. What is a Democrat? What is a Republican? As mentioned before, a Democrat is a person who is registered as a Democrat. A Republican is a person who is registered as a Republican. That's about as much logic as you'll get from anyone. This is not to say that most people don't have their reasons for belonging to either party. Nor is it to say that it is not important. It is important. A vote is a vote for whatever reason it is cast.

So, it works out that when a fellow wants to run for the presidency, he hovers under the banner of some party. Since each party can only be represented by one person in the general election, it usually works into a problem for the Democratic and Republican parties since each usually has more than one person trying for the job.

Now this eliminating process would be quite simple if the Democrats and Republicans each could, with a pencil, simply cross out the names of the candidates they didn't like or they thought didn't have much of a chance to win. However, our system of government is built on fairness, and that wouldn't be fair. Actually there are only two ways that those lists of would-be Presidents can be whittled down to one Democrat and one Republican.

Way No. 1

The applicant can withdraw of his own accord. This usually happens when the applicant (for one reason or another) simply decides that he can't pull enough votes to win.

Way No. 2

Each party can have an election and cut the list of would-be Presidents down to one Democrat and one Republican. (See sketches 27 & 28)

The above-mentioned elections take place at national conventions. In the summer of each election year, the Democrats have a get-together in one of our bigger cities. It is called the Democratic National Convention. Along about the same time, the Republicans have their get-together. It is called the Republican National Convention.

It would seem that that's fair enough if every citizen in our country is somehow (either directly or indirectly) allowed to take part in the above-mentioned elections. Most of us will ask, "How could every one of us have a say in who runs for the job of being our President?"

Here is the way it is. Every state in the Union sends representatives (called delegates) of its people to the Democratic National Convention. It is at this convention that a Democrat is selected (by getting the most votes) to represent the Democratic Party in the general election for the President of the United States.

Also, every state in the Union sends representatives (called delegates) of its people to the Republican National Convention. It is at this convention that a Republican is selected (by getting the most votes) to represent the Republican Party in the general election for the President of the United States.

The number of delegates that go to the Democratic National Convention is determined by the Democratic Party.

The number of delegates that go to the Republican National Convention is determined by the Republican Party.

The next thing we need to think about is how the delegates are chosen. Here is the way it is done. There is no uniform way of

CANDIDATES

DEMOCRATS

ONLY ONE CAN RUN
IN THE GENERAL ELECTION

Sketch 27.   The would-be Presidents can be cut down two ways...
(1) Withdraw of his own accord. (2) By party elections.

CANDIDATES

REPUBLICANS

ONLY ONE CAN RUN
IN THE GENERAL ELECTION

Sketch 28.   The would-be Presidents can be cut down two ways...(1)
Withdraw of his own accord. (2) By party elections.

selecting delegates to the Democratic and Republican National Conventions. Some states leave the selection of delegates to the Democratic and Republican Parties. However, most of the states hold primary elections.

Note: The word "primary" means first. It is the first election, to be followed by the general election.

While the above-mentioned Democratic and Republican primaries are determining who will go to the conventions, they are also used to determine local issues of one kind or another. Then, too, would-be Presidents (candidates) can (and often do) enter these state primaries simply to determine how they stand. In other words, if they don't make a good showing, they drop out.

Note: Actually, what we have been saying in the above portion of this chapter is that, just before election time, the Democratic and Republican Parties, each at separate conventions, with delegates from every state in the Union, determine who will represent them in the general election for the President of the United States.

CHAPTER 26

The National Conventions

To the student: A word about committees. Most of us have very limited experience with committees. For example, we have perhaps witnessed a teacher appointing a committee of two to collect money for a school picnic. In other words, we think of a committee as being composed of a few people who are occasionally appointed to perform a task for a bigger group.

In government, we find that most every job is done by a committee. Furthermore, we find that government committees are often composed of many people. So, it is not unusual if we, at first, find ourselves a little confused.

We are now about to outline, to some degree, the mechanics of how the national conventions operate. In other words, we will describe what takes place at the conventions. First, let us review with some questions.

Who sponsors the conventions? The Democratic Party sponsors one. The Republican Party sponsors the other.

What are the conventions for? One is to elect a would-be President for the Democrats. The other is to elect a would-be President for the Republicans.

Who attends the conventions? Elected (and other) Democrats from each state and territory attend one. Elected (and other) Republicans from each state and territory attend the other. The above-mentioned people from each state and territory are called delegates.

How many people attend the conventions? They run into

the thousands.

Why so many? There are so many because they represent millions of people.

Above we mentioned the people who attend the conventions. The next thing we need to know is, who runs the conventions? Who's the boss? What kind of an organization do they have? Well, here's the way it is.

The Democratic and Republican conventions are not exactly alike. However, they are enough alike that the same description pretty well fits both of them.

The conventions are held every fourth year. However, the organizations are kept intact between elections. The high authorities in each party are the delegates from each state who meet at the national conventions, which are held in the summer of the election year.

Each party's delegates elect a national committee. The committees are made up of two or more people from each state. Each of the committees is made up of several hundred people.

To the student: It is worthwhile to hesitate here for a second to help us understand what the Democratic National Committee and the Republican National Committee mean. You could say the Democratic National Committee is the National Democratic Party. You could say the Republican National Committee is the National Republican Party. In either party, when anything is done on a national basis, the above-mentioned committees are involved. You will be reminded of this time and again in the newspapers and on television.

Each party's national committee picks a national chairperson. This chairperson has charge of the presidential campaign. He appoints an executive committee to run the business of the party during the years between elections.

The most important thing that has to be decided by the National Committee (of each party) is where the convention is to be held. Another thing to be decided is the dates of the conventions. Other things that have to be taken care of are the rules of the conventions, the platforms and so on.

There is considerable interest in where the conventions are to be held. No one knows for sure, but the thinking is that if the meetings are held in the right city, it will somehow pull votes for the party.

Another thing, the conventions have to be held in cities that are big enough to accommodate the crowds that attend. There have to be adequate hotel rooms. There have to be enough restaurants to feed the people.

The mayors and the city fathers of most of the big cities put up a fight to have the meetings in their cities. Why? It's money. So many people flood the place with money.

These affairs last perhaps four or five days. They are fun occurrences. Some people go for football, some go for baseball and some go for tennis. There's a goodly crowd that goes for politics.

The chairman of the National Committee takes over the leadership of the convention. Committees are formed and voted into office.

The most important part of each convention is in the choosing of the party's candidate for President. The name of each state is called (a lengthy process), giving each one a chance to nominate its choice. The first round of voting then begins. If no majority is reached, a second roll call is made, followed by a second round of voting. This process is continued until there is a majority. Then the winner makes an acceptance speech. During this speech, the would-be President makes known his choice of a would-be Vice-President.

Definitions:

A *platform* is a list of what a candidate would do if elected.

A *plank* is part of the platform.

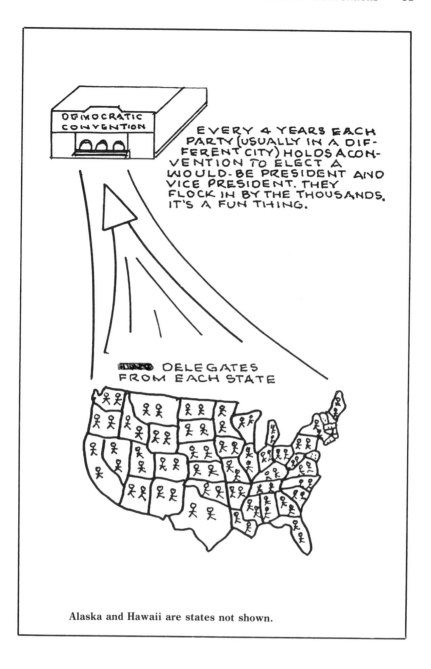

Alaska and Hawaii are states not shown.

CHAPTER 27

The
Vice President

The Vice President is nominated by the members of the party at a national convention. He is usually someone who is suggested by the presidential nominee. Where he is from usually has something to do with the selection. If the party needs votes in the area where he is from, his chances of being nominated are strengthened.

Most of us know little about the Vice President. We have to stop and think to recall his name. Up until a few years ago, the jobs he was assigned were not very important. You could say he was just there. He was standing ready to take over the big job in case something happened to the President. That has been changed.

The Constitution states that he shall be President of the Senate with no right to vote unless there is a tie. It also states that the Senate shall have another president of the Senate (called President pro tempore) in readiness in case the Vice President is absent. Actually, the Vice President is out of town quite a bit of the time.

Besides the above-mentioned duties, the Vice President takes part in the Cabinet meetings and is a strong link between the President and the Senate. He is also a member of the National Security Council.

It is probably by choice that the Vice President stays in the background. However, he knows what's going on. (See sketch 29)

Note: The Vice President receives about $79,125 per year, free housing and $10,000 a year for expenses.

VICE PRESIDENT AT WORK

PRESIDES OVER
SENATE MEETINGS - VOTES
IN CASE OF TIE

TAKES PART IN
CABINET MEETINGS

MEMBER OF NATIONAL
SECURITY COUNCIL

LINK BETWEEN
PRESIDENT AND SENATE

Sketch 29. Also, you could say the Vice President is a "trouble shooter" for the President.

CHAPTER 28

The Senate (Upper House)

The Senate is a group of one hundred people who make laws. They are elected, two from each state. The Senate meets Jan. 3 every year. The term of office is six years. Only one third of them is elected every two years. This keeps experienced people on the job all of the time. They are elected in November in even-numbered years. (See sketch 29A)

The President of the United States can call a meeting of the Senate when he thinks it's necessary.

Members of the Senate usually roost pretty high on the social and economic ladder. Most are well educated. They have the unique privilege of establishing their own salary. They make about $1,400 per week. The Vice President of the United States is president of the Senate.

A Senator must be at least thirty years old, must have been an American citizen for at least nine years, must be a resident of the state from which elected, and may not hold any other federal office while serving in the Senate.

Other than the basic rules listed above, it's almost impossible to list the things that enable a Senator to get elected. However, things like looks, education, ability to speak in public and money are bound to make a difference.

In reality, a Senator's appearance, ability to speak well and use of the mass media will also have a tremendous impact on his ability to be elected. With all factors considered, the voters have the final say.

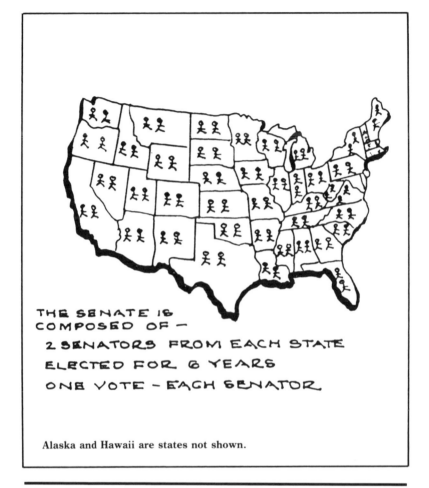

THE SENATE IS
COMPOSED OF —

2 SENATORS FROM EACH STATE

ELECTED FOR 6 YEARS

ONE VOTE — EACH SENATOR

Alaska and Hawaii are states not shown.

Sketch 29A.   It is well to keep in mind that for a bill to become law, it has to be passed by both the House of Representatives and the Senate.

The states with small populations were afraid that the states with large populations might control Congress and pass laws that the smaller states did not like. So it was decided that every state, no matter how small, would have two Senators. Then the Senators from the small states could vote together and defeat an unfair bill passed by the House of Representatives, in which the large states had more members.

The two Senators from a state are never up for election at the same time unless retirement, resignation or death occurs.

CHAPTER 29

Structure
Of The Senate

Now, we come to the structure of the Senate. But, what is "structure" in this case? It's how it's put together. There are one hundred people from all over the country whose job it is to make laws. Picture that many people in one room — who is boss? Who runs the works? To make it more confusing, the one hundred people are divided. Some are Democrats. Some are Republicans.

Here's the way it is. No decision has to be made as to who stands up front, whacks the table with the gavel and says "Come to order!" That decision was made back home when we elected the Vice President of the United States. It's the law. He is always the president of the Senate. Sometimes he's a Democrat and sometimes a Republican. He is called the presiding officer. You could say the presiding officer runs the meeting but does not take an active part in the lawmaking. He can only vote when there is a tie. After all, he is not a lawmaker. He's not a senator.

So, that leaves one hundred senators to make the laws. Some are Democrats, and some are Republicans. Here's what happens. The Democrats need an organization all their own to promote their interests. (See sketch 30) The Republicans need an organization to promote their interests. (See sketch 31) So, each party meets separately and elects officers to head the party and battle for votes when the lawmaking process is in operation.

The party organizations are alike. Here's how each is set up. We have mentioned the presiding officer. He presides over the one hundred senators — Democrats and Republicans.

Under the presiding officer, each party has:
... Floor Leader
   He is the main force in organizing the party.
   Schedules the work to be done.
   Promotes attendance on the floor.
   Collects and distributes information.
   Persuades other senators to adhere to party policies.
   He keeps in touch with the White House.
... A Policy Committee
   It works closely with the floor leader, whip and Policy Committee chairman to obtain its objectives.
... The Whip
   His job can be likened to a bird dog. He sniffs out who is to vote for whom.
   He questions, cajoles and turns on the charm to do what he can to help the floor leader.

Note: A *lame duck Congressman* is one who is serving the last session of his term. In other words, a lame duck is a Congressman who has been defeated but still is serving.

SENATE STRUCTURE - MORE DEMOCRATS

100 SENATORS

PRESIDING OFFICER → V.P. OF U.S.

DEMOCRATS

REPUBLICANS

FLOOR LEADER

FLOOR LEADER

POLICY COMMITTEE

POLICY COMMITTEE

WHIP

WHIP

HOUSE KEEPERS
= SECRETARY OF SENATE
= SERGEANT AT ARMS
= CHAPLAIN
= SECRETARY FOR REPUBLICANS
= SECRETARY FOR DEMOCRATS

= DEMOCRAT
= REPUBLICAN

Sketch 30. The "stickmen" at the top of the sketch represent the 100 lawmakers of which the Senate is composed. The blue ones are Democrats. The black ones are Republicans. Under the senators, we show the presiding officer, the Vice President of the United States.

Under the Vice President, we show the senators separated. The group on the left is Democrat. On the right are Republicans.

One will note, the Democrats have a floor leader, a Policy Committee and a whip.

One will note, the Republicans have a floor leader, a Policy Committee and a whip. Each party has its own organization.

In the lower right corner we show what we call "housekeepers." The housekeepers are not senators. They are important officers who serve to keep the lawmaking process in operation. They are usually given their jobs by the party that has the most members (the majority party). They are formally approved by both parties.

As mentioned before, we make no attempt to show the quantity of lawmakers in any of the above groups or committees. We do show (and this is important) by color which party has the most members. In other words, at a glance we can tell in any group which party has the power. So, let's take a look at the sketch and see what it tells us.

In the top of the sketch, there are more Democrats. They have the "say-so."

One will note, the structure of each party is alike. However, the Democratic floor leader is the one we read about and the one we see on television. Where does he get his power? His party has the most members and the most votes.

Note: No attempt is made to show the quantity of people in the sketch.

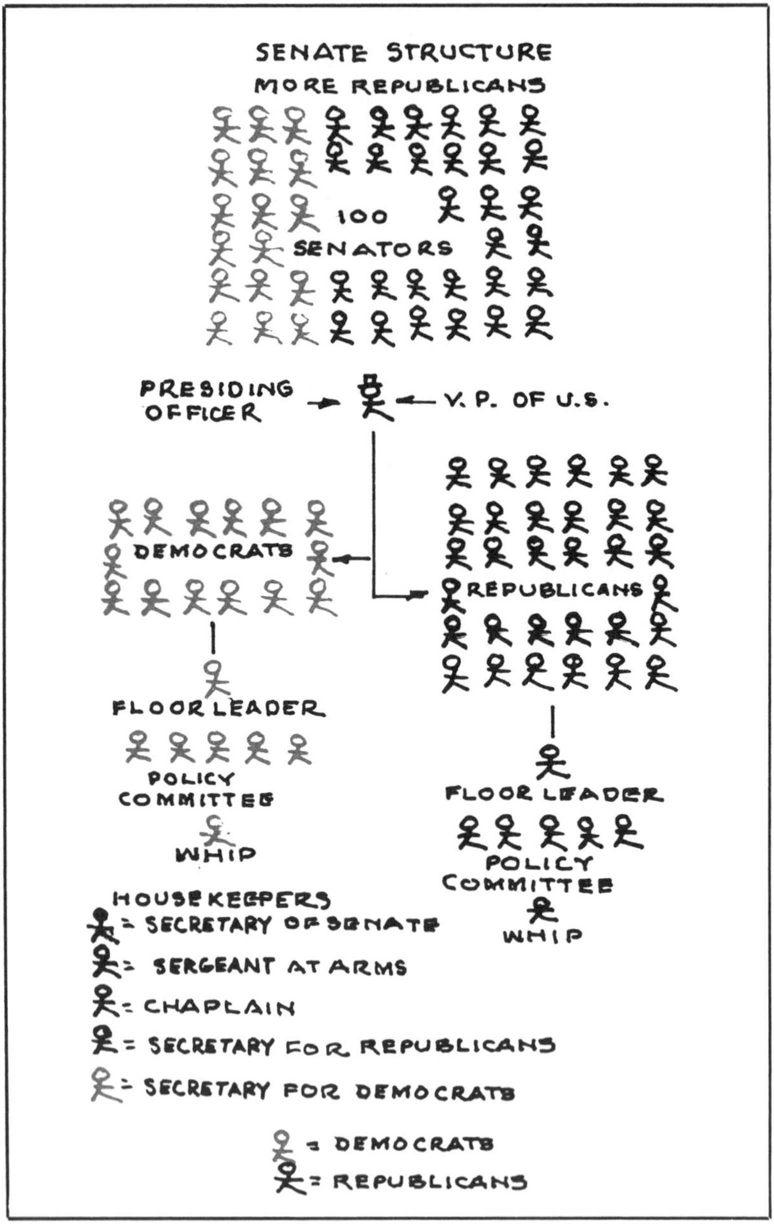

SENATE STRUCTURE
MORE REPUBLICANS

100 SENATORS

PRESIDING OFFICER → ← V. P. OF U.S.

DEMOCRATS → REPUBLICANS

FLOOR LEADER

POLICY COMMITTEE

WHIP

FLOOR LEADER

POLICY COMMITTEE

WHIP

HOUSEKEEPERS
= SECRETARY OF SENATE
= SERGEANT AT ARMS
= CHAPLAIN
= SECRETARY FOR REPUBLICANS
= SECRETARY FOR DEMOCRATS

= DEMOCRATS
= REPUBLICANS

Sketch 31.   The "stickmen" at the top of the sketch represent the 100 lawmakers who comprise the Senate. The blue ones are Democrats. The black ones are Republicans. Under the senators, we show the presiding officer, the Vice President of the United States.

Under the Vice President, we show the senators separated. The group on the left is Democrat. On the right are Republicans.

You will note, the Democrats have a floor leader, a Policy Committee and a whip.

You will note, the Republicans have a floor leader, a Policy Committee and a whip. Each party has its own organization.

In the left lower corner we show what we call "housekeepers." The housekeepers are not senators. They are important officers who serve to keep the lawmaking process in operation. They are usually given their jobs by the party that has the most members (the majority party). They are formally approved by both parties.

As mentioned before, we make no attempt to show the quantity of lawmakers in any of the above groups or committees. We do show (and this is important) by color which party has the most members. In other words, at a glance we can tell in any group which party has the power. So, let's take a look at the sketch and see what it tells us.

In the top of the sketch, there are more Republicans. They have the "say-so."

You will note, the structure of each party is alike. However, the Republican floor leader is the one we read about and the one we see on television. Where does he get his importance, his power? Here's where. His party has the most members and the most votes.

CHAPTER 30

How A Candidate Is Selected

Sometime before election day, most of us know who the candidates[1] are. We also know what they are running for. Sometimes it's for mayor, governor or perhaps the President of the United States. What most of us don't know is how the candidates were selected. Here's the way it is. There is some difference in the state laws. However, there are four methods that just about speak for any of the states. They are as follows:

A. For some local jobs, the would-be candidate simply files a petition[2] signed by a number of voters.

B. Sometimes a candidate may be selected in a meeting of party members, called a caucus.

C. Office seekers can be selected at nominating conventions.

D. The candidate can be selected in a primary[3] election. (See sketch 32)

Note: When political parties first started, would-be presidents and vice presidents were selected by lawmakers in party meetings. Later, the people became dissatisfied with that method. They said it was not democratic. In the election of 1832, each of the parties used national nominating conventions to select the candidates for the presidency and the vice presidency.

---

[1]A candidate is one who seeks office.
[2]A petition is a "formal request."
[3]Primary means "first."

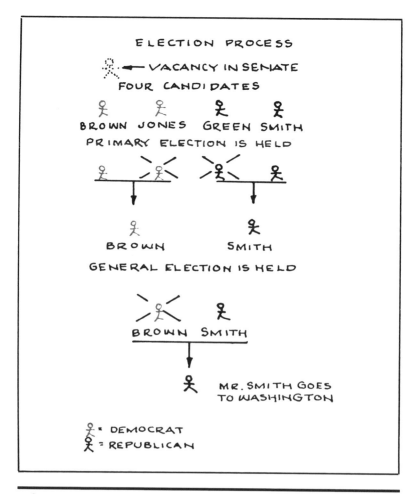

Sketch 32.   Let's pretend there's a vacancy in the Senate. There's just the one job open. That job is represented by the dotted figure at the top of the page. Under the above-mentioned figure you will see four people who are making a "try" for the job. You will note that Brown and Jones are Democrats, and Green and Smith are Republicans.

To eliminate one Democrat and one Republican, a primary election is held. Jones and Green were eliminated. That leaves Brown and Smith to "fight it out" in the general election.

You will note that Brown was eliminated in the general election. Mr. Smith goes to Washington.

CHAPTER 31

A Senator's Problems Back Home

It should be kept in mind that each state is represented by only two people in the Senate. Those people have a lot of territory to think about when a bill is submitted for their approval.

Just about all the states have several major industries and a lot of small industries that could be adversely affected if the wrong bill is made into law. (See sketch 33)

Note: A senator's concern is mostly in the area of lawmaking. However, it is well to bear in mind that his group has some special powers (though seldom used) that are very important. (See sketch 34)

Filibuster and Cloture

Filibuster

A filibuster can be likened to the action of a 3-year old who points to a cookie jar and yells and yells and yells until someone hands him the jar. Here's the story:

Senate Rule 22 provides for unlimited debate on a bill before it can be voted on. Consequently, sometimes a senator takes the stand and talks and talks and talks (on just about any subject) until the opposition gives in to him. People get tired and worn out. They are anxious to get on with other work. Finally, they let the talker have his way.

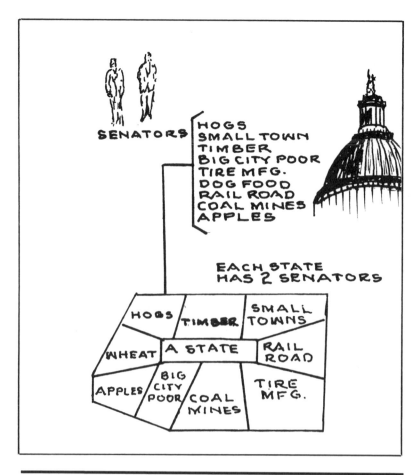

Sketch 33.   At the bottom of the above sketch there is a make-believe state. It is to help us keep in mind that there is a lot of territory for two senators to represent in Washington. The state has been divided into areas showing the various industries. In other words, it shows how people make a living in various parts of the state. The upper part of the sketch shows a list of the products and industries. Also mentioned is the big city poor and small towns that add to the worries of the two senators.

Senators have to pretty well keep track of what's going on back home to make sure the interests of the people who voted for them are well taken care of in Washington.

ONLY THE SENATE CAN

1 APPROVE OR REJECT MAJOR AP-
POINTMENTS MADE BY THE PRESI-
DENT.

2 RATIFY TREATIES.

3 ELECT A VICE PRESIDENT FROM TOP
CANDIDATES IF THERE IS A TIE IN
THE ELECTORAL COLLEGE.

4 TRY GOVERNMENT OFFICERS FOR
CRIME.

Sketch 34.   For the most part, a senator's job is to make laws. However, he has some special powers (though seldom used) that are very important.

Note: Ratify means to approve.

Cloture (or closure)

Cloture is a rule in the Senate that can be used to limit debate or break a filibuster. Here's how:

One-sixth of the Senate can formally request the Senate to close debate on the subject at hand. If the request is approved by two-thirds of the senators voting, no senator can speak for more than an hour on the bill.

CHAPTER 32

The Senate's Standing Committees

Sometimes it seems like just about everyone in the country has a bill they want passed. Before a law is passed it is called a bill. There are thousands of bills that pour into Washington every year.

Some of the bills are good, some bad, and many not even worth considering. Those that are worth considering require a lot of thought and a lot of research. It is to be remembered that the bills made into laws are the very rules by which we live. They can affect our lives in many ways.

Some laws tend to work to the advantage of some groups of people and to the disadvantage of other groups of people.

When you stop to think about it, it is obvious that endless confusion would occur if one hundred people tried to do the research and study required on each bill.

This is the way it is handled. Members of the Senate are separated into nineteen smaller groups. These groups (in their own way) get off to themselves and work on the bills assigned to them. (See sketch 35)

The above-mentioned groups are called *standing committees*. The size and purpose of the committees remain pretty much the same year after year. However, the membership often changes after an election.

The committee on Rules and Administration has much say-so on when (and if) bills reach the Senate for discussion and vote.

Members of the standing committees have a varied amount of power and prestige.

```
        STANDING COMMITTEES
              SENATE

AGING
AGRICULTURE, NUTRITION AND FORESTRY
APPROPRIATIONS
ARMED SERVICES
BANKING, HOUSING AND URBAN AFFAIRS
BUDGET
COMMERCE, SCIENCE AND TRANSPORTATION
ENERGY AND NATURAL RESOURCES
ENVIRONMENT AND PUBLIC WORKS
ETHICS
FINANCE
FOREIGN RELATIONS
GOVERNMENTAL AFFAIRS
HUMAN RESOURCES
INTELLIGENCE
JUDICIARY
RULES AND ADMINISTRATION
SMALL BUSINESS
VETERANS AFFAIRS
```

Sketch 35.   Let's make sure we understand what "Standing Committees of the Senate" means. To begin, what is a committee? A committee is a small group of people appointed to do a job for a bigger group.

The "Senate" is a group of 100 people from which the committees are selected.

The word "standing" means that these committees are pretty much permanent. In other words, they have been in use for several years. For the most part, each name gives a clue to the nature of the bill that is assigned to it. In other words, the "Small Business" committee tells us that the bills assigned to it pertain to small businesses.

That brings up a good question. How are the members elected? Here's the way it is done.

Two groups of people make the choices: Republican Conference Committee and Democratic Steering Committee. By tradition the Senate accepts what the two committees have decided.

One thing you can depend on — if there are more Republicans than Democrats in the Senate, the chairperson and most of the members of the standing committees will be Republicans. Of course, the reverse is true if most of the members are Democrats.

CHAPTER 33

Checking Our Progress

To the student: Sometimes we get involved in the study of the details of our government and lose track of the over-all picture that we are trying to get in mind.

Let us keep in mind:

There are only three parts (branches) as mentioned above.

We have studied:

The President and the Senate.

We have yet to study the House of Representatives and the Supreme Court. (See sketch 36)

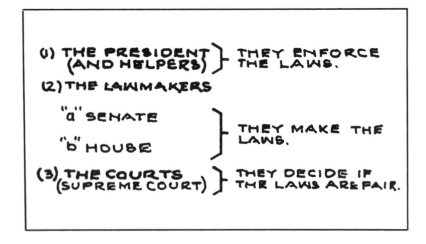

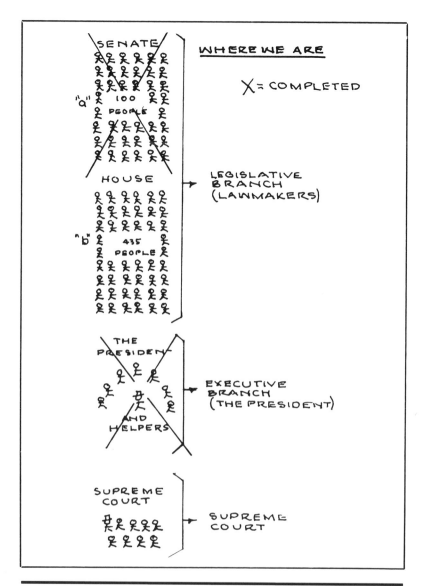

SENATE
"a" 100 PEOPLE

HOUSE
"b" 435 PEOPLE

WHERE WE ARE

X = COMPLETED

LEGISLATIVE
BRANCH
(LAWMAKERS)

THE PRESIDENT
AND HELPERS

EXECUTIVE
BRANCH
(THE PRESIDENT)

SUPREME
COURT

SUPREME
COURT

Sketch 36. The above is to remind us that of the three parts that make up the United States government. We have studied one and one-half of them. They are crossed out above.

CHAPTER 34

The House Of Representatives (lower house)

The House of Representatives is a group of four hundred thirty-five (435) people who make laws. Why four hundred thirty-five? Here's the story.

Years ago when there weren't many states, few representatives were needed. However, as our population grew and when more states were added, more representatives were needed. That worked out fine for a while, but finally, as more and more states were added, there were so many people milling around up there it became cumbersome. As it worked out, the figure was permanently set at four hundred thirty-five in 1929.

That presented a problem. What part of the four hundred thirty-five would be allotted to each state? Then, too, what would be done when new states were added? The problem was solved by making an adjustment after each decennial[1] census. The adjustment was made by allowing each state a portion of the four hundred thirty-five representatives based on the state's population relative to the population of the whole country.

To be sure that every state in the Union has at least one representative in the House of Representatives, each state is first allotted one member. That leaves 385 (435 − 50 = 385) seats. The remaining 385 seats are then fairly allotted to the states on the basis

---

[1]A decennial census is a counting of the people that takes place every ten years. It takes place in the years that end in zero.

AFTER 1980 CENSUS
NUMBER OF REPRESENTATIVES
(EACH STATE)

ALABAMA	7	MONTANA	2
ALASKA	2	NEBRASKA	3
ARIZONA	3	NEVADA	2
ARKANSAS	4	NEW HAMPSHIRE	2
CALIFORNIA	45	NEW JERSEY	14
COLORADO	6	NEW MEXICO	3
CONNECTICUT	6	NEW YORK	34
DELAWARE	1	NORTH CAROLINA	11
FLORIDA	19	NORTH DAKOTA	1
GEORGIA	10	OHIO	21
HAWAII	2	OKLAHOMA	6
IDAHO	2	OREGON	5
ILLINOIS	22	PENNSYLVANIA	23
INDIANA	10	RHODE ISLAND	2
IOWA	6	SOUTH CAROLINA	6
KANSAS	5	SOUTH DAKOTA	1
KENTUCKY	7	TENNESSEE	8
LOUISIANA	8	TEXAS	27
MAINE	2	UTAH	3
MARYLAND	8	VERMONT	1
MASSACHUSETTS	11	VIRGINIA	10
MICHIGAN	18	WASHINGTON	8
MINNESOTA	8	WEST VIRGINIA	4
MISSISSIPPI	5	WISCONSIN	9
MISSOURI	9	WYOMING	1

ONLY THE HOUSE OF REPRESENTATIVES CAN

(1) ORIGINATE MONEY BILLS.

(2) ELECT A PRESIDENT FROM THE TOP CANDIDATES WHEN NONE RECEIVE OVER HALF OF THE ELECTORIAL VOTES.

(3) DECIDE IF A GOVERNMENT OFFICER SHOULD BE TRIED FOR A CRIME.

Sketch 37.   For the most part, a House member's job is to make laws. However, he has some special powers (though seldom used) that are very important.

Note: The above "originate money bills" means that when money has to be raised for something, the proposal to raise it has to start in the House. Only then can the Senate vote on it.

of their population. In other words:

$$\frac{\text{Population of state}}{\text{Population of country}} \times \frac{385}{1} = \text{number of representatives}$$

Note: The above formula is not to imply that this is the exact way it is figured. Several formulas have been used.

The House of Representatives meets Jan. 3 every year. Representatives are elected every two years. Elections are held in November of even-numbered years. As a rule, representatives are well-educated. They come from occupations such as business, law, teaching and agriculture.

Members of the House of Representatives establish the amount of their own salary. Other allowances are made to cover their expenses. Then, too, some of them make money writing for magazines and making speeches. Their regular pay is about $1,400 per week.

We now come to the question of how the members of the House of Representatives are elected. They are elected in most states the same way the senators are. It is to be noted that when anyone wants to run (get his name on the ballot) for office, he has to submit a specified number of signatures of registered voters to an appropriate official. This, in a way, proves that the candidate is serious about making a try for the job.

The House of Representatives is composed of 435 members whose job is to make laws. There are Democrats and Republicans. How is the place run? Who's the boss? Well, here's the way it's handled. The Democrats have an organization all of their own. The Republicans have an organization all their own. After an election and they all get settled in Washington, each party goes off by itself and elects its officers.

Qualifications:

A House member must:

be 25 years old,

live in the state he represents and

be a citizen of the United States for at least seven years.

House members have some important but seldom-used powers. (See sketch 37)

CHAPTER 35

Structure Of The House Of Representatives

Now we come to the structure of the House of Representatives. How does it operate? It is to be kept in mind, there are four hundred thirty-five people sent to Washington from all over the country. Their job is to make rules by which all of us live. Since there are so many members, who's the boss? There are Democrats. There are Republicans. Who is in charge? (See sketch 38 & 39)

Note: Please keep in mind that "majority party" means the party with the most members.

Listed below are the people who "run the show."

Majority Party	Minority Party
Presiding officer (speaker of the House)........................	
Floor leader	Floor leader
Policy Committee	Policy Committee
Whip	Whip

To the student: The above list, with the "Majority Party" and "Minority Party," can be a little confusing. The presiding officer has another name. Some people say presiding officer. Some say the speaker and some say Mr. Speaker. It's a good idea to understand that he is the fellow who is the boss of the meeting regardless of the term used to refer to him.

Please bear in mind that the Democrats have a floor leader, a Policy Committee and a whip, and the Republicans have a floor leader, a Policy Committee and a whip.

No doubt each party would like to have a presiding officer. However, two people can't conduct a meeting. So what happens? The party with the most members (the majority party) gets the job.

Below are some of the jobs that the floor leaders, Policy Committees and the whips do.

The Speaker (the presiding officer)

He is the most influential House officer. He conducts the meetings. He handles the little wooden hammer. His importance comes from the fact that he can decide who does and who does not get to speak from the House floor. He can simply fail to call on people who are not "on his side." To get the job, he has to be a member of the majority party. Then, too, he has to be liked by the members of his party. They have a meeting, and he is voted into the job. He is then formally approved by the House of Representatives.

Floor Leader

There are two floor leaders. The Democrats have a floor leader. The Republicans have a floor leader.

The functions of a floor leader are as follows:

1. He organizes the party.
2. He schedules the work to be done.
3. He fights for attendance on the floor.
4. He sees that the members are informed.
5. He sees that the members stick to party policies.
6. He stays in touch with the White House.

Policy Committee

There are two policy committees. The Democrats have a Policy Committee. The Republicans have a Policy Committee. They work closely with the floor leader and whip to obtain their objectives.

The Whip

There are two whips. The Democrats have a whip. The Republicans have a whip. His job can be likened to a bird dog. He sniffs out who is to vote for whom. He questions, cajoles and turns on the charm to do what he can to help the floor leader.

HOUSE STRUCTURE
(MORE REPUBLICANS)

435
HOUSE MEMBERS

PRESIDING OFFICER → ☺ ← SPEAKER

DEMOCRATS → | → REPUBLICANS

FLOOR LEADER

POLICY COMMITTEE

WHIP

FLOOR LEADER

POLICY COMMITTEE

WHIP

HOUSE KEEPERS

☺ = CLERK   ☺ = PARLIAMENTARIAN

☺ = DOOR KEEPER   ☺ = SERGEANT AT ARMS

☺ = POSTMASTER   ☺ = CHAPLAIN

Sketch 38. The "stickmen" in the top part of the sketch represent the 435 members of the House of Representatives. The blue ones are Democrats. The black ones are Republicans. Below we are showing the presiding officer. He is also referred to as the speaker. Below the speaker we show the House members separated. The group on the left are Democrats. The group on the right are Republicans.

You will note the Democrats have a floor leader, a Policy Committee and a whip.

You will note the Republicans have a floor leader, a Policy Committee and a whip. Each party has its own organization.

Other than the lawmakers we have mentioned above, there are what we refer to as "housekeepers." They are not lawmakers. However, they have important jobs that contribute a lot to the lawmaking process. Their jobs are as follows: a clerk, parliamentarian, doorkeeper, sergeant at arms, postmaster and chaplain. They are appointed by the majority party and formally approved by both parties.

At a glance at the sketch we can tell which party has the power. As always, it's the one with the most members. The most members means the most votes. The speaker is the important person. He is the one we read about in the newspapers. Why? He has control of the party with the most votes. For the same reason, the Republican floor leader is a very important person.

Note: No attempt is made in the sketch to show the actual quantity of House members. We do, however (with color), show the majority party in any group. Majority party means the party with the most members.

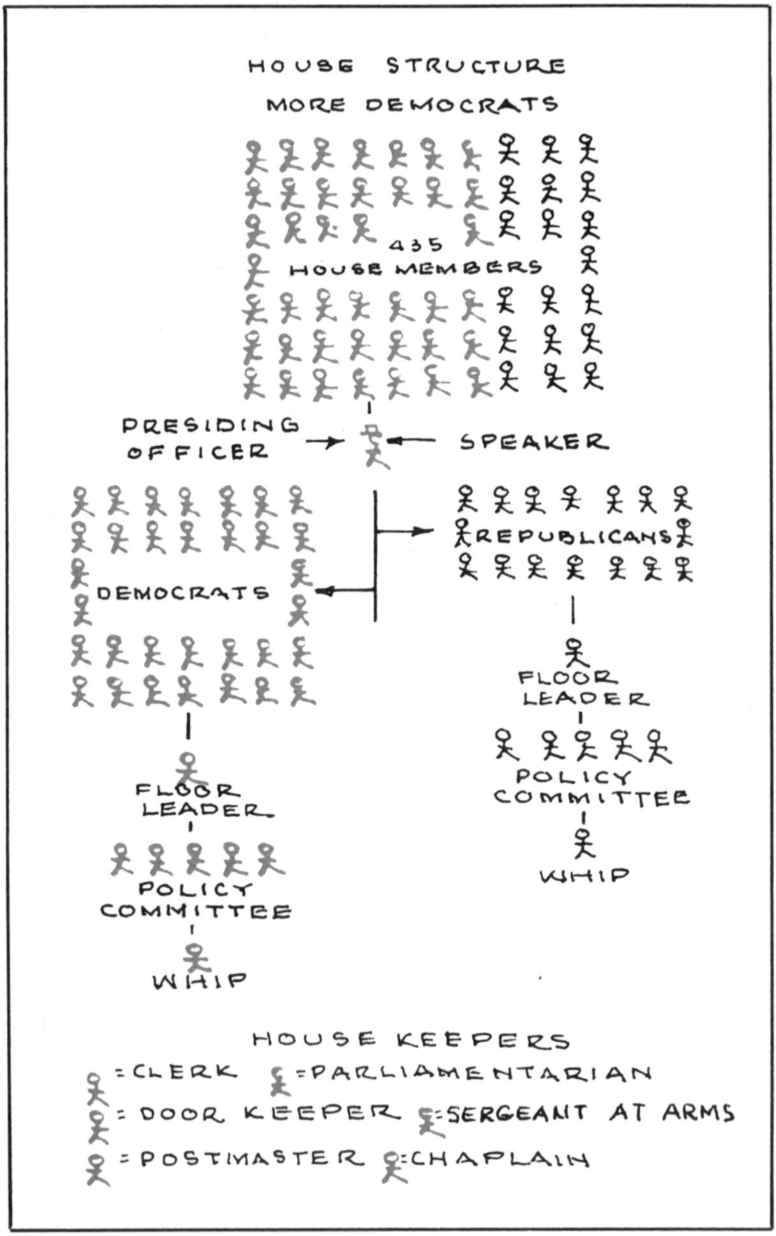

HOUSE STRUCTURE

MORE DEMOCRATS

435 HOUSE MEMBERS

PRESIDING OFFICER → ← SPEAKER

REPUBLICANS

DEMOCRATS

FLOOR LEADER

POLICY COMMITTEE

WHIP

FLOOR LEADER

POLICY COMMITTEE

WHIP

HOUSE KEEPERS

= CLERK   = PARLIAMENTARIAN

= DOOR KEEPER   = SERGEANT AT ARMS

= POSTMASTER   = CHAPLAIN

Sketch 39.   The "stickmen" in the top part of the sketch represent the 435 members of the House of Representatives. The blue ones are Democrats. The black ones are Republicans. Below we are showing the presiding officer. He is also referred to as the speaker. Below the speaker we show the House members separated. The group on the left are Democrats. The group on the right are Republicans.

You will note, the Republicans have a floor leader, a Policy Committee and a whip.

You will note, the Democrats have a floor leader, a Policy Committee and a whip. Each party has its own organization.

At a glance at the sketch we can tell which party has the power. As always it's the one with the most members. The most members means the most votes. The most votes means the speaker would be a Democrat. Since the speaker runs the meetings and can get things done for his party, he is a very important person.

CHAPTER 36

Apportionment — Gerrymandering

You could say that apportionment is drawing lines on a state map that show the area that is represented by each lawmaker in the House of Representatives. It is the law that each of the areas shall contain the same amount of people. (See sketch 40)

Apportionment is necessary because without it the states would become over-represented or under-represented, as a result of people moving around.

The job is done after each decennial census. In other words, every ten years the Census Bureau counts the people and tells each state the number of representatives it can have in the House of Representatives. The state lawmakers then draw the lines.

By using census records, drawing the lines that separate a state into districts (that contain the same amount of voters) is not a very difficult task. It can be done (within reason) a number of different ways.

Usually the party in power draws the lines. Of course, they are familiar with where the pockets of their followers are located. Using this information, they locate the districts where it is an advantage to their party when the voting takes place. This is called gerrymandering. (See sketch 41)

Note: It is to be noted that each state is first allotted one representative regardless of population. What's left from the 435 that are allowed is apportioned, according to population, among the states.

Note: Sometimes *apportionment* is called *districting*.

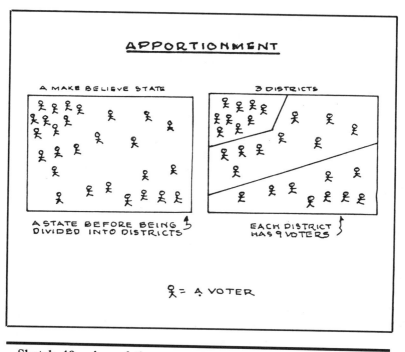

Sketch 40. Any of the states that we could pick to show what apportionment is would involve figures into the millions. So, to make it easier, we are using a make-believe state.

Here is the situation:

This small state received word (after the decennial census) that it has 27 residents and is entitled to three representatives. That means each representative would represent nine people.

The top, left map shows the location of the 27 residents. The map at right shows that the lines have been drawn showing three districts of nine people each. That's what apportionment is.

To the student: We have learned that apportionment is drawing lines on a state map that show the area represented by each lawmaker in the House of Representatives.

Now...let's make sure we understand *why* these lines are drawn. Here's why. It's to make sure that each representative represents the same amount of people. But, we could ask, is that important? It is, because it's fair.

To give an example, it certainly wouldn't be fair to have one man represent two people and another represent one hundred people.

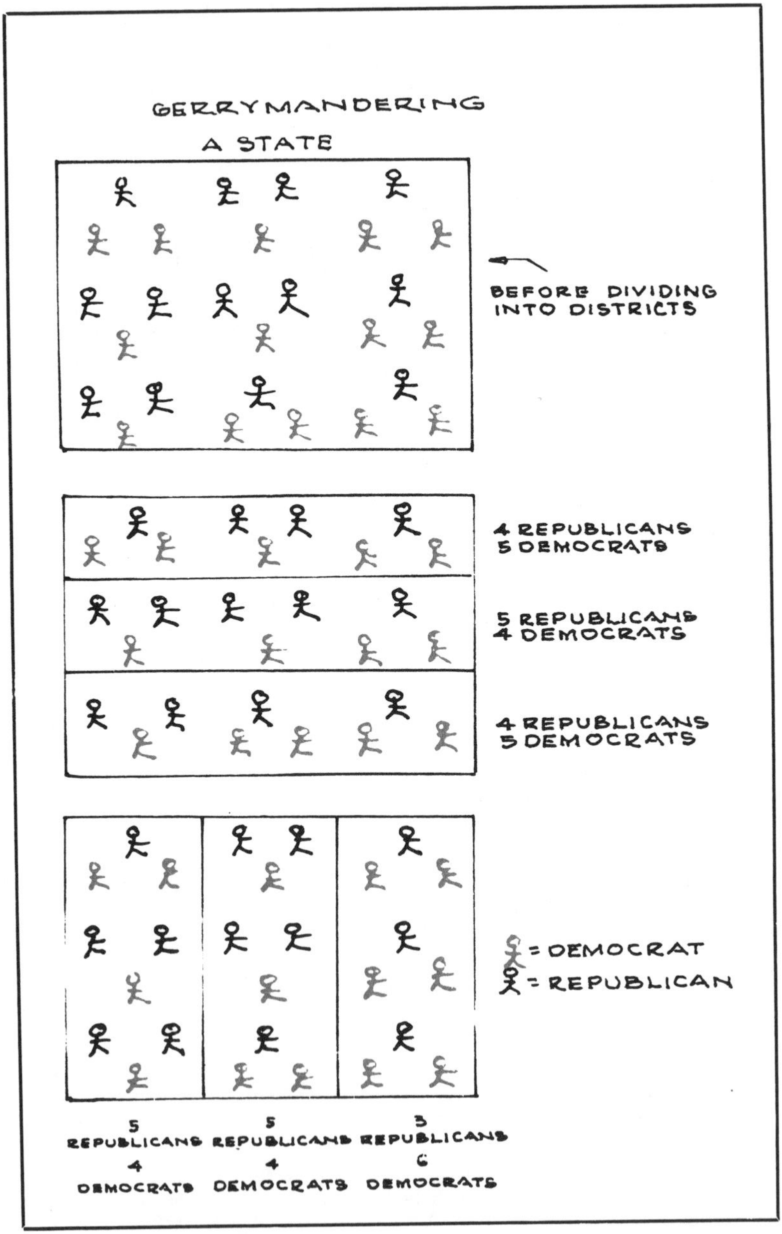

GERRYMANDERING
A STATE

BEFORE DIVIDING INTO DISTRICTS

4 REPUBLICANS
5 DEMOCRATS

5 REPUBLICANS
4 DEMOCRATS

4 REPUBLICANS
5 DEMOCRATS

= DEMOCRAT
= REPUBLICAN

5
REPUBLICANS   REPUBLICANS   REPUBLICANS
4   4   6
DEMOCRATS   DEMOCRATS   DEMOCRATS

Sketch 41. Any of the states we could pick to show what gerrymandering is would involve figures into the millions. So, to make it
easier, we are using a make-believe state. Here's the situation:
This small state has received word (after the decennial census) that
it has 27 residents and is entitled to three representatives. That means
that each representative would represent nine people.
It so happens that 13 of the people are Republicans and 14 are
Democrats. Now, if the Democrats happen to be in power, they could
divide the state as shown in the middle figure. By counting the
Democrats and then counting the Republicans, you will note that two
of the districts would "go Democratic" and one district would "go
Republican."
If the Republicans happened to be in power they could divide it as
shown in the bottom figure. By counting the Democrats and then counting the Republicans, you will note that two of the districts would "go
Republican" and one would "go Democratic."
The above-described process of drawing the boundaries (of election
districts) to give one party an advantage is called gerrymandering.
Now, we have described what gerrymandering is; let's be sure we
understand just what it amounts to when it takes place. The lines in
the middle figure are placed so that more Democrats live in two of the
districts. More Republicans live in one of the districts. Obviously, this
means that two Democrats and one Republican would be elected.
The lines in the bottom figure are placed so that more Republicans
live in two of the districts. More Democrats live in one of the districts.
Obviously, this means that two Republicans and one Democrat would
be elected.

CHAPTER 37

Problems Back Home (The House)

Most of us never get to really know a member of the House of Representatives. We just pull a lever or mark a check mark by their name and that's about it. One thing they do is to look out for our interests in Washington. For example, if the people in the area he represents make their living raising potatoes, you can bet if a bill comes up that could affect the sale of potatoes, our representative will be in there fighting for us. (See sketch 42)

Congress
What does the word "Congress" bring to mind? The dictionary definition is "a meeting together of persons."

In government circles it depends on who's talking and who's listening.

To most people it means the House of Representatives and the Senate.

To some it means only the House of Representatives.

To some it means "a bunch of people up there in Washington who make the laws."

Perhaps it will be helpful if a little explanation is made. In the first place, let's ask a question. Why is the word "Congress" used? Why not say the "House of Representatives and Senate." The answer is simple enough. Congress is shorter. Using shorter words saves space. They're thought of as being one because each is involved in the process of making laws.

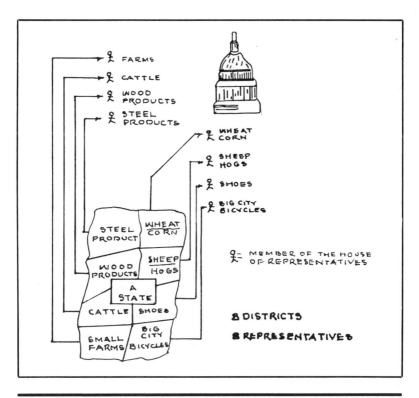

FARMS

CATTLE

WOOD PRODUCTS

STEEL PRODUCTS

WHEAT CORN

SHEEP HOGS

SHOES

BIG CITY BICYCLES

STEEL PRODUCT

WHEAT CORN

WOOD PRODUCTS

SHEEP HOGS

A STATE

CATTLE   SHOES

SMALL FARMS

BIG CITY BICYCLES

♀ = MEMBER OF THE HOUSE OF REPRESENTATIVES

8 DISTRICTS

8 REPRESENTATIVES

Sketch 42.   You will remember that all states do not have the same number of members in the House of Representatives. You will remember, too, that the number of members is based on the population of the state relative to the population of the United States. On that basis, this make-believe state in the above sketch had enough population to be allowed eight members.

Each of the eight members is from a different district. But what's a district? A district is part of the state that (at least in theory) has been divided so that each representative has an equal portion of the population in the state he represents. The lines in the above sketch show the district of each of the eight members of the House of Representatives.

Also, we have (in the sketch) labeled the main thing that brings money into the district. And, of course, that's the thing about which your representative has to know a lot and be concerned.

You will note that we have written "city" in some of the spaces. That's because so much of the member's time is taken up with problems of the big city.

CHAPTER 38

The House's Standing Committees

There are 435 members in the House of Representatives. With that many people representing millions of people scattered over the 50 states, one can't help but wonder what kind of a setup they have to get their work done in an orderly manner. This is the way it is. The House of Representatives is divided into committees. Most of the committees are considered permanent. They are called standing committees. The number has varied from time to time. At present there are 23. (See sketch 43)

It is to be noted that the standing committees are very powerful. Here's why. Each bill, through an established procedure, finds its way to one of the standing committees. The committee that it is assigned to can either:

kill it (simply file it), or

give it an OK to be presented to the House for debate.

Many bills assigned to the standing committees are killed. Even so, so many "get by" that it is impossible (due to the time it takes) for the House to consider. Consequently, the number of bills that reach the House has to be cut down to a manageable amount.

This job is done by the Rules Committee. Here is the way it is. All bills that "get by" any of the standing committees have to be okayed by the Rules Committee. That makes it the most powerful of any of the standing committees. In other words, this committee has the capacity to sift out any bill it doesn't like.

As mentioned above, the standing committees are powerful. They can affect our lives in many ways. That brings up a good question.

STANDING COMMITTEES (HOUSE)

AGRICULTURE
APPROPRIATIONS
ARMED SERVICES
BANKING, HOUSING AND
URBAN AFFAIRS
BUDGET

DIST. OF COLUMBIA
EDUCATION AND LABOR
FOREIGN AFFAIRS
GOVERNMENT AFFAIRS

HOUSE ADMINISTRATION
INTERIOR AND INSULAR AFFAIRS
INTERSTATE AND FOREIGN COMMERCE
JUDICIARY

MERCHANT MARINE AND FISHERIES
POST OFFICE AND CIVIL SERVICE
PUBLIC WORKS AND TRANSPORTATION
RULES

SCIENCE AND TECHNOLOGY
SMALL BUSINESS
STANDARDS OF OFFICIAL CONDUCT
VETERANS AFFAIRS
WAYS AND MEANS

Sketch 43.   As important as the committees are, they cannot "pass" a bill. They can research, debate, file, stall and so on. However, a bill has to get the most votes in both the Senate and House to become law.

COMMITTEES OF THE

HOUSE OF REPRESENTATIVES

= DEMO.
= REPUB.

435 PEOPLE

BUDGET   JUDICIARY   RULES

POST OFFICE-   WAYS AND   VETERAN'S
CIVIL SERVICE   MEANS   AFFAIRS

SCIENCE AND   EDUCATION   GOVERNMENT
TECHNOLOGY   AND LABOR   AFFAIRS

HOUSE ADMIN-   ARMED   HOUSE AD-
ISTRATION   SERVICES   MINISTRATION

Sketch 43A. The top part of this sketch indicates the House of Representatives. Also shown are some of the committees. The objective of the sketch is to help us remember that the party that has the most members in the House always winds up with the most members on each of the committees. Also you will note the chairman (wearing the hat) belongs to the party with the most members. The party with the majority of members in the House can choose the majority of committee members.

How are the members selected?

Here's the way it is. Two groups of people make the choices: one group (Democratic Steering Committee) are Democrats; the other (Committee on Committees) are Republicans. What they decide is later presented to the whole House for ratification. By tradition, the House accepts what the two committees have decided.

You can bet on it, if there are more Democrats than Republicans in the House, most of the members and the chairmen of all of the standing committees will be Democrats. Of course, the reverse is true when there are more Republicans in the House.

Special Committees

It is well to keep in mind that for a bill to become law, it has to be okayed by the Senate and House of Representatives. For that reason it is sometimes necessary to form special committees. One of them is called a joint committee.

A joint committee is made up of members of both the Senate and the House of Representatives. By working together, both houses of Congress can save time and not duplicate each other's work.

CHAPTER 39

Getting Bills Passed

Starting in the
House of Representatives

A House member (no one else) may introduce a bill in the House of Representatives. A member gets his bill typed and puts it in a box (called a hopper) beside the clerk's desk. There is a routine procedure the bill goes through. It is given a number, the title is recorded, it is printed in the government printing office and made available to the House members. (See sketch 44)

Most of the time, the bill is assigned to a committee by the Speaker of the House. The bill is placed on the committee's calendar. The action of the committee has a lot to do relative to whether the bill has a chance of becoming a law. You could say that all but the most important bills are screened out. There are subcommittees. Some bills are passed on to them for research and study. Private citizens can testify about a bill if they want to. Most bills, before they become law, have a number of amendments tacked onto them.

Bills are placed in three categories after they are reported favorably by a committee:

1. Union calendar — bills concerning money.
2. House calendar — public bills not pertaining to money.
3. Private calendar — private bills.

When a bill is being considered by the House, each member is privileged to speak for one hour. Lots of debating goes on. When the debating is finished, a vote is taken. There are four ways of voting on a bill.

1. the voice vote,
2. division vote — voters stand and are counted,
3. a teller vote — voters walk by a teller who does the counting,
4. roll call vote — each member says "for" or "against" as his name is called.

The Senate

The procedure in the Senate is pretty much as it is in the House. One difference is that a senator must be recognized by the presiding officer.

Once a bill is introduced, it is numbered and the title recorded. The bill is referred to a committee, which is about the same treatment that it gets in the House.

When a bill passes the two houses in different forms, a conference committee made up of members from each house is often used to reconcile the differences.

After a bill has been passed by both the House and Senate, it goes to the President for his approval. He can act in one of three ways:

1. He can sign the bill; it becomes law.
2. He can veto the bill. In that case, he writes a statement explaining what's wrong with it. Then the bill goes back to the House of its origin. It then can only become law if both Houses pass it with a two-thirds vote.
3. The President can simply refuse to act on the bill. At the end of 10 days (not including Sundays) the bill then becomes law without his signature if Congress is still in session. If Congress has adjourned, the bill does not become law. This is known as a pocket veto.

Note: There are times when there is some variation from the above. The above is to give a general understanding of what takes place.

Pressure Groups — Lobbyists

Groups formed for the purpose of changing government policies are called pressure groups. They are often sponsored by labor unions, big companies and other organizations.

GETTING BILLS PASSED

Sketch 44.   This sketch is to help us get an understanding of what takes place when a bill is made into law.

1 — House member presents bill to House of Representatives.
2 — House speaker gives bill to House committee.
3 — Committee gives bill back to full House.
4 — Bill moves from House to Senate.
5 — Presiding officer in Senate gives bill to committee.
6 — Committee gives bill back to full Senate.
7 — Senate gives bill to President.
8 — President signs bill; it becomes law.

Note: A bill can be presented in either the House of Representatives or the Senate. However, all bills for the raising of revenue must begin in the House of Representatives.

There are, at times, conditions that prompt some variation in the above outline. However, the sketch should bring to mind the general routine of what takes place.

A person belonging to a pressure group is referred to as a lobbyist. A lobbyist is usually a well-informed person, a good talker and a charming person with money to spend. His job is to pull votes favored by his sponsor.

Lobbyists are legally required to register, telling who they work for, their pay and the like.

Note: The word "veto" means "power of forbidding."

CHAPTER 40

The
Supreme Court

First, what is the meaning of Supreme Court? That is, what do the words mean? Well, here it is.

The word "supreme" means holding highest authority. The word "court" means "a legal group that defends the rights of others." So it follows that the Supreme Court is a group of people with the highest authority that defends the rights of others.

Now, the next thing that enters the mind is, what is this "rights of others" that's mentioned above? That's simple enough. It's the basic laws of the United States Constitution. However, that's not the whole story. The real authority comes from the people. It's our willingness to accept the rules as they are written.

It can be compared to a family. If the kids in the family are not willing to live by the rules as they are laid down by the mother and dad, the family is headed for trouble. But, of course, the rules have to be fair. That's where the Supreme Court comes into play. It makes that judgment. Always they answer the question: Is it fair? Perhaps it will be worthwhile to mention how the court works.

There are nine people. One of the nine people of the court is called the Chief Justice. The other eight people are known as associate justices. The Supreme Court makes judgments on cases that can't be settled in the lower courts. There are two exceptions:

a. cases involving foreign officials

b. cases involving state governments

The Chief Justice assigns responsibility for writing the opinions to the other justices.

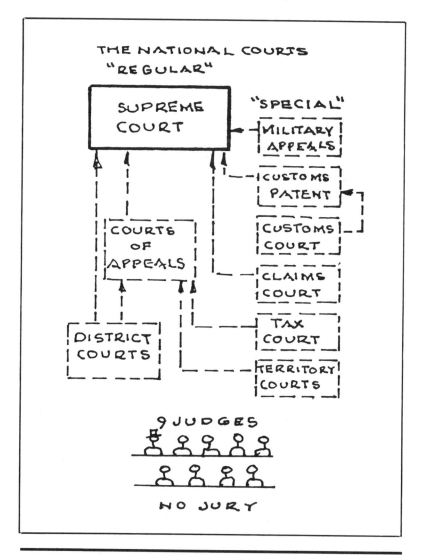

Sketches 45A & 45B.   The nine rectangles at the top represent all of the national courts. The darkened rectangle represents the one we are now learning about...the Supreme Court.

The bottom sketch is to remind us (at a glance) that the Supreme Court is composed of nine judges (no jury).

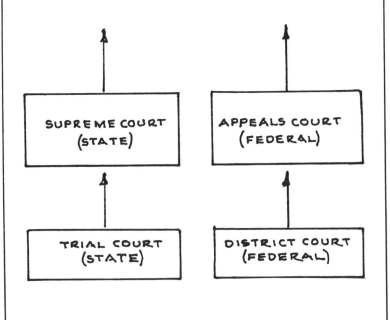

TWO ROADS TO SUPREME COURT

UNITED STATES SUPREME COURT

SUPREME COURT (STATE)	APPEALS COURT (FEDERAL)
TRIAL COURT (STATE)	DISTRICT COURT (FEDERAL)

Sketch 45C.   The United States Supreme Court accepts cases from either state or federal courts.

Note: Opinions in this case means their reasoning relative to their decisions.

The justices of the Supreme Court are appointed by the President and have to be approved by the Senate. They keep their jobs for life. Their salaries cannot be lowered as long as they are in office. The associates make about $8,400 per month. The Chief Justice makes about $8,725 per month.

When the Court meets in session, all of the justices sit together at the same time. However, not every justice has to be present at every court session. A simple majority of the justices hearing a case is necessary for a decision.

A court term begins on the first Monday in October and continues for as long as necessary to get the work done. They usually finish about the middle of June. The Court works in a very methodical manner. It meets every two weeks in public sessions to hear arguments. It then spends a couple of weeks studying the arguments in order to arrive at a decision for each case that has recently been heard.

The decisions and the opinions of the Supreme Court are important to many lawyers scattered around the country. The Supreme Court's line of reasoning is especially valued. There is often more than one opinion written for a case. Of course, there is always the majority opinion that gives the opinion and reasoning of most of those who support the majority decision. A justice who does not agree with the majority often writes a dissenting opinion. A justice who agrees with the Court's decision, but not with the reasoning by which it was reached, often prepares a concurring opinion.

CHAPTER 41

The National Courts

We are not about to study the courts in the colonies or the states. We've done that. We are now about to study the national courts. (See sketch 46)

But, just what are the national courts? National pertains to the nation, the whole country. You could say the "United States courts."

Just why do we have "national courts"? They exist because the job the national courts do cannot be done by the state courts. The national court is a higher court. But what is a higher court? "Higher" in this case means more authority. Now, the next question that comes up is, why can't the state courts handle any case? Well, here is an example. Suppose there is an argument about where the boundary line is between two states. It is obvious that a case of this kind would have to be tried in a higher court.

Another example would be when one state dumped its sewage into a river that flowed into another state. Again, it is obvious that a higher court is a necessity.

Our national court system has nine kinds of courts. You could say the purpose of all of them is the same. It's to settle arguments. People disagree. Who is right? Who is wrong? That's just about what it amounts to.

We have nine different kinds because the disagreements that courts settle are varied. A thorough understanding of each court, therefore, should include learning about the functions of each. The more one learns about courts, the less complicated they seem.

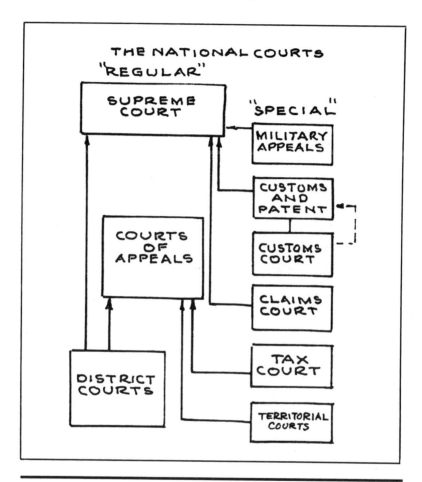

Sketch 46.   The above nine rectangles represent the nine courts that make up our national court system. You will note the three rectangles on the left side of the sketch are marked "regular." That is because those courts are the most used. They are the courts that most of us are (more or less) familiar with. They are the ones we read most about in the newspapers.

The six rectangles on the right marked "special" represent courts that are more able to handle cases of a special nature. You will note the name of the court gives an idea as to the nature of the cases handled. The arrows indicate where the cases can be tried for the second or third time if conditions warrant.

CHAPTER 42

District Courts

A district court is a national court that serves a certain area. The size of the area depends on how thickly it is settled. Every state has at least one district court. Some have as many as four.

The district court is described as a general trial court and is sometimes called a superior or circuit court.

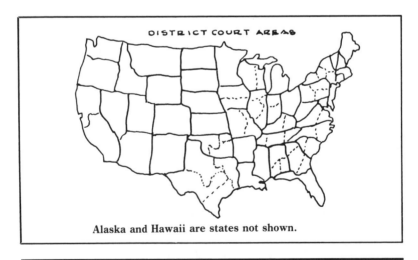

DISTRICT COURT AREAS

Alaska and Hawaii are states not shown.

Sketch 47A.   The sketch shows all the districts in the United States. Where the states have more than one district, it is shown with dotted lines.

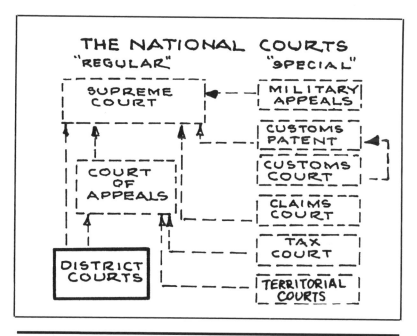

Sketch 47B.   The nine rectangles in the sketch represent all of the national courts. The darkened rectangle represents the one we are now learning about — the district courts.

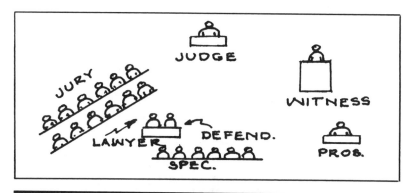

Sketch 47C.   You will note from the sketch, it is much like the lower state courts. There is a judge (elected), jury, witnesses, defendant, defense and prosecuting attorneys, and so on.

CHAPTER 43

Court
Of Appeals

First, what is the meaning of the term "Court of Appeals"? Well, the word "appeal" means "asking for assistance." And that is pretty well what anyone does when they take a case to the court of appeals. Actually the court of appeals is a higher court in the national court system where anyone can take a case when he is dissatisfied with a decision made in a lower court.

There are eleven courts of appeals. Each one serves in a certain numbered area.

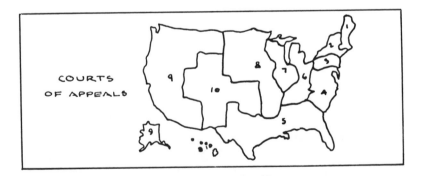

Sketch 48A. The court of appeals areas are shown. No cases originate in the court of appeals. Appeals courts take cases from the district courts in their area. Like the Supreme Court, there is no jury. The court of appeals settles cases that the Supreme Court does not have time to handle.

Sketch 48B.   The nine rectangles in the sketch represent all of the national courts. The darkened rectangle represents the one we are now learning about — the court of appeals.

Sketch 48C.   The sketch was made to remind us that the decisions are made by three judges in a panel.

CHAPTER 44

Court
Of Military Appeals

Due to its nature, this court operates as a part of the Department of Defense. However, that has nothing to do with the decisions it makes. The court of military appeals consists of a chief judge and two associate judges. This court acts as an appeal court on cases from the military courts. It operates in Washington, D.C. (District of Columbia).

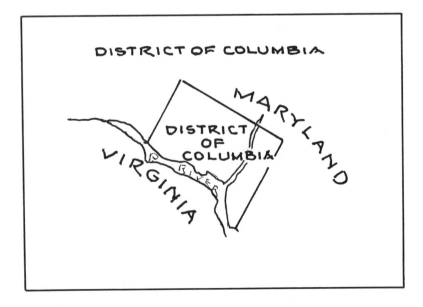

Sketch 49B.   The nine rectangles in the sketch represent all of the national courts. The darkened rectangle represents the one we are now learning about — the court of military appeals.

Sketch 49C.   The sketch was made to help us note (in a glance) that the court is made up of three judges.

CHAPTER 45

Court Of Customs
And Patent Appeals

The court of customs and patent appeals has to do with cases that can't be settled in the customs court and also in the field of patents and trademarks. There is a chief judge and four associate judges. Other than the above-mentioned judges, there is a clerk, a marshal, a reporter and their assistants. Decisions in this court can be reviewed by the Supreme Court. The court of customs and patent appeals is in Washington, D.C. (District of Columbia).

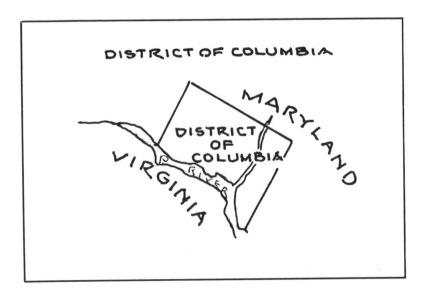

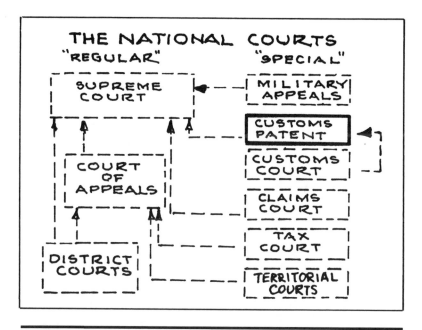

Sketch 50B.   The nine rectangles in the sketch represent all of the national courts. The darkened rectangle represents the one we are now learning about — the court of customs and patent appeals.

Sketch 50C.   The purpose of the sketch is to (at a glance) remind us that this court has five judges to make the decisions. The judges sit together in a panel. They operate in Washington, D.C.

CHAPTER 46

The Customs Court

This court has to do with many things relating to the entry of goods into the United States from foreign countries. The customs court is made up of a chief judge and eight associate judges. It also has a staff of clerks and marshals.

There are nine judges who sit in groups of three at ports of entry. The main office is in New York City.

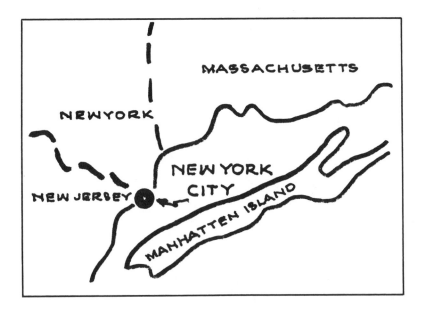

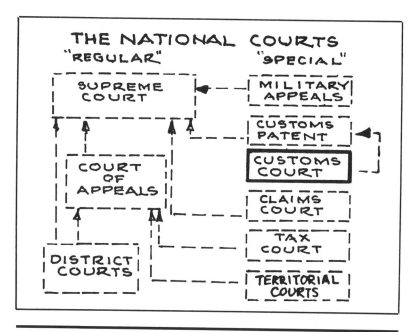

Sketch 51B.   The nine rectangles in the sketch represent all of the national courts. The darkened rectangle represents the one we are now learning about — the United States customs court.

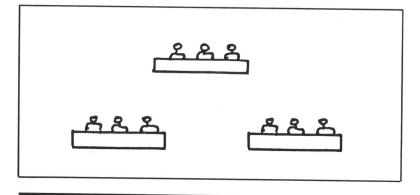

Sketch 51C.   In the sketch we have shown three groups of three judges to remind us (at a glance) of how many judges there are and that there are three panels in different places.

CHAPTER 47

Claims Court

The court of claims is the court you would go to if you wanted to sue the United States government. For example, if you owned a farm that the government needed and refused to pay you what you figured it was worth, the court of claims is the court you would go to to get a fair hearing.

The court of claims is made up of a chief judge and six associate judges. They all sit together in a panel to hear a case. There are a number of other people who belong to the staff of the court.

The court of claims also hears appeals from Indian tribes relative to the decisions of the Indian Claims Commission.

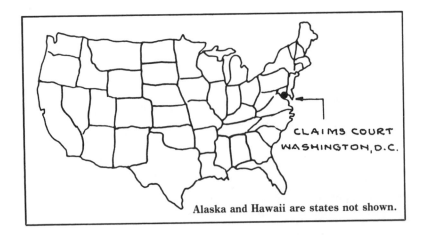

CLAIMS COURT
WASHINGTON, D.C.

Alaska and Hawaii are states not shown.

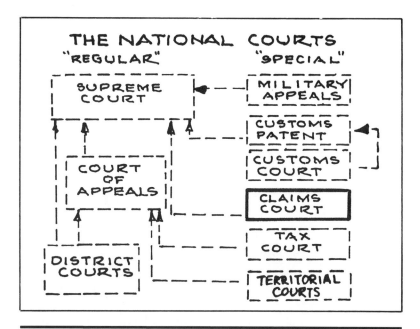

Sketch 52B. The nine rectangles in the sketch represent all of the national courts. The darkened rectangle represents the one we are now learning about — the United States court of claims.

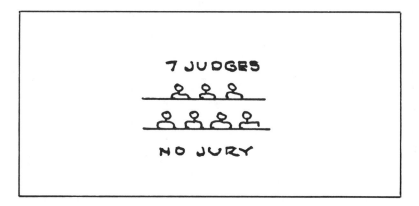

Sketch 52C The sketch was made to help us note (at a glance) that the court is made up of seven judges who sit together to form a panel.

CHAPTER 48

Tax
Court

The tax court is the place a person goes when he thinks the United States government is charging him too much in taxes. The court is made up of sixteen judges. The judges, appointed by the President and okayed by the Senate, are scattered around the country. It makes a convenient way for a person to get a hearing when he is dissatisfied. If he still isn't satisfied after a hearing, he can take his case to the court of appeals.

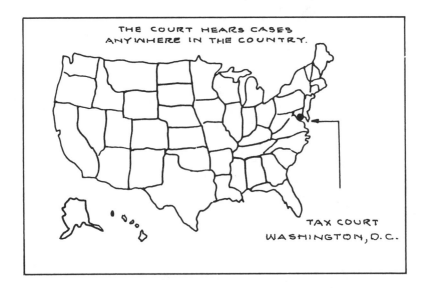

THE COURT HEARS CASES ANYWHERE IN THE COUNTRY.

TAX COURT
WASHINGTON, D.C.

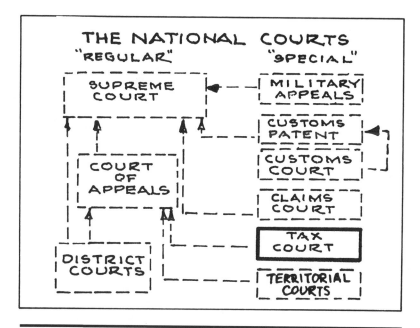

Sketch 53B.   The nine rectangles in the sketch represent all of the national courts. The darkened rectangle represents the one we are now learning about — the tax court of the United States.

Sketch 53 C   The sketch represents the 16 judges. This sketch is simply to remind us (at a glance) that the tax court is operated by 16 judges scattered at convenient locations around the country.

CHAPTER 49

Territorial Courts

The territorial courts are courts established by Congress in Puerto Rico, the Virgin Islands, the Panama Canal Zone and Guam. Three judges serve on the court in Puerto Rico, two in the Virgin Islands, one in the Panama Canal Zone and one in Guam. Judges on these courts are appointed for terms of four to eight years.

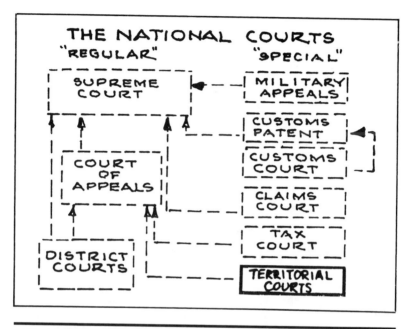

Sketch 54B.   The nine rectangles in the sketch represent all of the national courts. The darkened rectangle represents the one we are now learning about — the territorial courts.

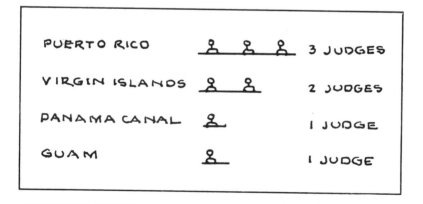

Sketch 54   The purpose of the sketch is to (at a glance) remind us of the number of judges in each of the territories.

CHAPTER 50

Voting

The Precinct
See Chapter 22.

Ballot
When the subject of voting comes up, you often hear the word "ballot." What is it? It is a slip of paper used in secret voting. A ballot box is a box with a slit in the top that you drop the ballot in after you have marked it.

Voting Methods
Quite often a machine is used instead of the ballot and box. You push a lever, and your vote is then counted and recorded. It saves time and keeps errors to a minimum.

Voting Place
The next thing that comes to mind is, where do we go to vote? It's usually in a public building, perhaps in a schoolhouse. It is best to have it near the center of the precinct where it is easy to get to. It's handy to have parking space nearby as most people vote soon after they leave their workplace.

The Sign
It's easy to spot where the voting is taking place. There's usually considerable activity around the building where the people go to vote. Almost invariably there is a fairly big sign posted that

BALLOT

CLASS PRESIDENT
MARK ONE ☒
JONES ☐ BROWN ☐

BALLOT BOX

VOTING BOOTH

IN THE BOOTH IS
THE VOTING MACH-
INE. IT COUNTS THE
VOTES.

VOTE
10

SIGN

has the word "vote" and the precinct number displayed.

Who Can Vote?

Can a person (when he/she reaches the age of 18) simply walk over to the voting place and vote? The answer is no. It's not that simple. Now, here's what he has to do. Of course, it varies some with each state.

First, he has to register. But what's that? Well, you could say it's "getting your name on the book." Actually, when you go in to vote, the first election worker you come to will ask your name. Then the worker will hunt for your name in a book. If the worker finds your name, that means you are registered. In other words, you can vote. If the worker doesn't find your name, that means you are not registered and cannot vote.

Usually you do not register in the same place where you vote. In the city hall (or another place) there is a registration clerk to whom you apply to get registered. The clerk will have you fill out and sign a printed form. The clerk will then give you a card that shows you are registered. That's all there is to it. The clerk places your name in a book that is sent to the precinct at election time.

Proof of Residence

In some states, to prove that the applicant is living in the precinct, the clerk routinely mails a card to the applicant's address. If the card is not deliverable (comes back), the applicant's name is removed from the book. He is no longer registered.

Length of Time Registration Lasts

In most states the above procedure makes the applicant permanently registered. Of course, if he moves, he must reregister in order to get his name moved to another precinct.

Qualifications

As a rule, one has to:

...be a citizen of the United States.

...be at least 18 years old.

...be registered.

...live in the district some specified length of time.

INDEX

For information about additional copies of this publication write:
Management Club Consultants
P.O. Box 460028
Garland, Texas 75046